A LIFE
WORTH
LIVING

A LIFE
WORTH
LIVING

SIR NICHOLAS SHEHADIE

SIMON & SCHUSTER
AUSTRALIA

A LIFE WORTH LIVING

First published in Australia in 2003 by
Simon & Schuster (Australia) Pty Limited
20 Barcoo Street, East Roseville NSW 2069

A Viacom Company
Sydney New York London Toronto

Visit our website at www.simonsaysaustralia.com

© Sir Nicholas Shehadie and Phil Tresidder 2003

Cataloguing-in-Publication data:

Shehadie, Nicholas, Sir, 1926– .
    A life worth living.

    ISBN 0 7318 1161 5.

    1. Shehadie, Nicholas, Sir, 1926– . 2. Mayors – New South
    Wales – Sydney – Biography. 3. Rugby football players –
    Australia – Biography. 4. Civic leaders – Australia –
    Biography. I. Tresidder, Phil. II. Title.

994.106092

Front and back cover photograph (on left) © Fairfax Photo Library
Typeset in Minion 11.5 pt on 18 pt by Letter Spaced
Printed in Australia by Griffin Press

For my grandchildren,
Persephone, Victoria, Nicholas, Francesca, Natasha and Edward

CONTENTS

ACKNOWLEDGMENTS

The writing of this book has been for me a journey of enriching revelation. It has been written for my grandchildren in the hope that they will learn from it something of their grandfather's early life.

I had always been reluctant to write an autobiography, but finally I agreed after much persuasion from many of my friends, as well as from strangers who had heard Sally Loane interview me on ABC radio after I retired as chairman of SBS in late 1999.

I have many people to thank for their support and their confidence in me. My thanks to Philip Tresidder for the his assistance in putting this book together, and also to Jacquie Brown of Simon & Schuster, who deciphered my handwriting and worked with me for many hours.

Thanks also to Dick Littlejohn, Roger Vanderfield, Norbert Byrne, John Howard (of rugby) and John Dedrick, who helped me recall various aspects of the struggle in establishing the Rugby World Cup, and to Trevor Allan for supplying me with important tour details.

I would also like to thank the late 'Pop' and Edith Thornley, who guided me early in my rugby career. Also Wally Meagher, the late Len Palfreyman, Don Walker, and Miss Harker, my kindergarten teacher. Appreciation to the late Sir Emmet McDermott, Leo Port and Andrew Briger, from my early days as a city councillor. I am indebted to Foss Van Breda, who assisted me in my early commercial life, and to John Utz, whom I count as a lifelong trusted friend.

In addition, I am indebted to the wonderful cardiac team at the Royal Prince Alfred Hospital, Sydney.

In particular, I wish to thank my sisters, Alice, Paulette and Margaret, and my brother, George. On many occasions, George acted as an anchor for me in business, which enabled me to spend time on the many activities I became involved in. I have always had the support of my three children, Michael, Susan and Alexandra, who were there whenever I needed them and who never failed to give advice or to debate an issue when our opinions differed.

What do I say about Marie, my wife for more than forty-six years and friend for fifty years? She has taught me much — not a day goes by that I don't learn from her. Highly intelligent, a free thinker and conversant in world affairs, she is a woman of great strength of character and compassion. When needed, she has always been there for me.

FOREWORD

I'm honoured to be asked by Sir Nicholas Shehadie to write a brief foreword to this book. His story, as told here, proves yet again that success is, more often than not, born of adversity; that there is no royal road to achievement or public prominence; that what people do with their lives is sometimes more noteworthy for the simplicity of its progress rather than the dimension of its achievements.

Nick Shehadie would say, in his usual self-effacing way, that there are many stories like this. And so there are. Yet the picture that emerges here, told so effortlessly and unpretentiously, has a magic of its own.

On reading of this life, you can't help but be engrossed by its difficulty and its dimension. A Lebanese boy of straitened means becomes a Wallaby lock, prop and captain, lord mayor of Sydney, and a distinguished public figure: Nick was the chairman of TAFE and chairman for nearly twenty years of the ethnic broadcaster, SBS. Nick is the first to say it's been a fortunate life. The fortune derives from his being born of Lebanese parents and reared, in his words, by 'a close-knit, caring family who endured much poverty in the Depression years in a new country'.

It is as if no one is more surprised by Nick's success than Nick himself, yet, emphatically, he has been its chief architect. Of course, sport, among other things, emancipates people; it frees their self-confidence and self-esteem. It evokes ambitions individuals dare not utter; and it places people in the most challenging peer group environment anyone could ever enter. Survive that and the path is so often much clearer. Nick Shehadie didn't just survive, he triumphed, stellar style.

I knew Nick well during my reign as Wallaby coach. He was the president of Australian rugby as we sought to climb off the bottom of the international ladder. No team and no coach could have had a more supportive, discreet, courteous, informed and understanding leader in what were often difficult times.

In more recent times, he has been chairman of the Trustees of the Sydney Cricket and Sports Ground Trust, of which I am a member. The leadership he offered, while often tested, never failed. In his quiet and dignified way, he dealt with those tempted to meddle with the history and tradition of two great sporting theatres, the Sydney Cricket Ground and the Sydney Football Stadium. Those people soon learned that the man at the head of the body, statutorily charged to manage them, was not to be messed with.

This book ploughs all of that soil. The reader will be carried along by the ease with which the story is told and by the unaffected way in which the subject of the story emerges from the anonymity of the back streets of Redfern to positions of real triumph in politics, sport, broadcasting and ethnic leadership.

By his example and by his making of something special in his own life, Nick Shehadie is, I am sure, at least indirectly, and perhaps more, telling young Australians from all walks of life to try as he has tried; to get up and go for it and ask the questions later. Right throughout this story, he seems to be urging those who might be inspired by its telling not to ask about the prize but, rather, enter the contest first.

He seems to be saying that with the right approach, the right attitude, the right spirit, a lot of elbow grease and some important but good-natured guidance, those who confront the vagaries of life are bound to find, as Sir Nicholas did, the journey much more rewarding and fascinating than the arrival.

In many ways, this story is, in the Australia of 2003, very much a text for the nation.

Alan Jones

PROLOGUE

A lone yacht climbed the peaks of the massive waves, then plunged with sickening impact into the cavernous, watery gorges below. The slender fibreglass boat was lost, isolated from the fleet of the 1970 Sydney–Hobart yacht race by an angry ocean and the howling gales that buffeted Bass Strait.

Was this adventure that I had anticipated so eagerly really *sport*, I wondered? Our lives were at risk, survival our desperate prayer. This was my introduction to ocean racing; hopefully, if I got out of it alive, it would also be my farewell to it.

The moon had fled and a coal-black curtain enveloped the sky. Our yacht, *Rum Runner*, was tossed like a cork in the billows, rain

The calm before the storm. A sunny, cheerful scene at Careening Cove wharf in Sydney Harbour as my daughter Alex farewells me. Soon afterwards we set out in *Rum Runner* to join the flotilla for the start of the 1970 Sydney–Hobart yacht race.

2

squalls lashing across the exposed deck. Yet the worst was still to come. At around ten o'clock in the evening, only our helmsman, John Byrne, was on deck, secured by a safety harness and wrestling grimly at the wheel. The rest of the crew was huddled below, where suddenly we experienced a frightening crash. I was thrown out of my bunk. Our boat had been knocked onto its side — the mast was lying in the water and waves were washing over the deck. John Byrne was badly bruised and suffered a broken rib. Jim Turner, rigger and a veteran waterman familiar with every inch of *Rum Runner*, thought we could have holed the boat, or maybe struck a whale. If the boat were holed, it would sink.

After the boat righted itself, we waited anxiously for daylight in order to inspect the damage. The bailing was frantic and we were waist-deep in water. We had no power; the sea had damaged everything. By early daylight, we had heaved to for the inspection and there was more frenzied bailing. Fortunately there was no hole, but with the waves continuing to crash over us we were drenched.

We managed to get going again, and headed for the closest point on the north-east coast of Tasmania, which we estimated to be at least 50 kilometres away. A small plane flew overhead, but it almost certainly didn't sight what must have been only a speck on the ocean. We felt we could make it if each man took hourly turns at the helm in the heaving seas.

The cruel misfortunes of *Rum Runner*, and the many other battered casualties of the 1970 fleet, came with little warning. We had departed Sydney Harbour on Boxing Day, in a traditional scene that must be just about the most spectacular in world sport. Hundreds of thousands of spectators lined the harbour shoreline, with thousands more positioning themselves on the rocky Heads that opened out into the high seas and the moody Tasman. The unfurling of colourful sails, the frenetic jostling for position and, finally, the salvo of the starter's gun and the exciting rush towards the Heads, was pure exhilaration for an amateur sailor such as myself.

So, what was *I* doing here — a sportsman with a rugby background, and a very definite sense of terra firma and, oh yes, at the time, Sydney's deputy lord mayor? In the early 1960s my friend Graham Nock, then managing director of the hardware chain Nock & Kirby and a colleague on the Sydney City Council, invited me to join his crew on a boat named *Alyth*. Sailing in the number-one division each Saturday from the Yacht Squadron at Kirribilli, at the northern end of the Sydney Harbour Bridge, was a novel experience for me, and one that I enjoyed very much. We had a great deal of success, and developed into an efficient and competitive crew. Soon afterwards, the renowned sail-maker Peter Cole designed a fibreglass ocean yacht to be named the Cole 43. He initially built three of them — *Taurus*, *Bacardi* and *Rum Runner* — and Graham, our skipper, purchased the last named, a beautiful, red-hulled boat that was to be my introduction to ocean racing.

After competing in many of the short overnight races, we were now ready to tackle the big event, the Sydney to Hobart classic, commencing on Boxing Day, 1970. Our crew consisted of Graham as the skipper, with Jim Turner as his right-hand man; Ron Smith and Harry Smith (no relation) and myself from *Alyth*; and John Byrne, Alex Scott and Geoff Manley, all of whom had previously crewed on Vic Meyer's famous yacht, *Solo*, and had much previous experience in the Hobart marathon.

Some two weeks prior to the Boxing Day departure we entered a return race to Lion Island, just north of Sydney in Pittwater. A southerly gale was blowing and we had *Rum Runner* planing on the huge seas — it was just like riding a surfboard — with the speedometer needle flat tack. Rounding Lion Island and beating back into the southerly, we took a pounding from the huge waves. When we were off Whale Beach, the aluminium mast snapped with an almighty bang and crashed onto the deck. It was all hands on deck trying to reassemble the gear that had become detached. We turned back, motored into calmer water and docked at Newport in Pittwater.

Our main concern was to have the boat restored for the Boxing Day start. It was a tight deadline, but Jim Turner worked non-stop, and at ten o'clock on the morning of the big race we had finally stepped the mast at Careening Cove in Neutral Bay. We made our way across to the starting line with little time to spare before the starter's gun went off. The bigger yachts immediately pushed through the field, and most of the fleet chose to go along the western shore of the harbour. We skirted along the eastern shore, which gave us a fantastic lift all the way. We only needed to tack once — on the mark at the Heads right in front of Sir Robert Creighton-Brown's *Pasha*, which would ultimately win the race. We were third out behind the leaders, surprising everyone. We set a spinnaker and carried it for about two and a half days down the New South Wales coast, having a beautiful ride almost to Bass Strait.

Pounded by monster waves, *Rum Runner* is down to its storm gear in Bass Strait with only one brave, lonely figure visible at the wheel on deck. The rest of the crew has sought refuge below.

According to radio reports, we were about the furthest boat out to sea, and from these reports we learned that a number of the competitors had withdrawn because the seas were becoming steadily bigger and more dangerous, and were causing severe gear damage. As we entered Bass Strait the waves were massive, so we immediately took the precaution of changing down to storm gear: a smaller mainsail and a very small jib. The pounding that *Rum Runner* had to take was frightening at times.

With the conditions too severe and the damage to the yacht after our capsizing too serious to continue racing, we limped to shore at a Tasmanian township called Bicheno. I had prayed during those lost nightmare hours in the storm that had nearly destroyed us, but I had such faith in our crew that I never said goodbye. Yes, I had been scared. The boat up-ending in the heaving seas and filling with water was a terrifying experience, all the more so because it happened so quickly. It was just like a car crash. But no one panicked, and we got out of it alive. When we reached shore, where a local fisherman presented us with fresh lobsters, I kissed the ground and decided there and then that I was cured of ocean racing!

Part One

A PRIVATE LIFE

1 THE EARLY REDFERN YEARS

I have had a most fortunate life, living with one foot in the Old World and the other in the New. I was the third child of Michael and Hannah Shehadie. My father, like his father, after whom I had been named, was a clergyman in the Antioch Orthodox Church. My grandfather was the first of the Shehadies to come to Australia, though it hadn't been exactly by choice. He arrived from Lebanon in 1910, aged in his early forties, having been turned out of his parish in Kousba, in the north of the country, after a serious disagreement with his bishop. Banishment to Australia was thought to be a suitable punishment for his stubbornness. My grandfather was a big man, very forceful, and with a reputation for not putting up with

The imposing figure of my grandfather, Nicholas Shehadie, resplendent in his religious regalia and decorations. He was head of the Antioch Orthodox Church in Australia and New Zealand and patriarch of the migrating Shehadies.

any nonsense. It was said that if a member of his congregation spoke or made any noise during his sermons, he would stride down from the pulpit and deliver them a hefty smack about the head. For many years after he arrived in Australia he lived alone, without the company of any members of his family, who had remained in Lebanon due to the outbreak of the First World War.

My father, Michael, one of seven children, was a studious and well-educated man; he was a graduate in chemistry and spoke several languages. In his late teens he had won a scholarship to the University of Kiev, then part of Russia, where he studied theology.

My parents had known each other as teenagers growing up in Kousba. My mother had an outgoing personality and had many suitors. My father was quiet and reserved — a gentle man. By the mid-1920s, now married and with two young daughters, my parents decided to migrate from Lebanon and join my father's parents and several of his brothers and sisters, who were now living in Australia.

Lebanese people began arriving in Australia in the mid-1800s, some apparently under the impression that they were bound for the United States, where a gold rush was in progress. What a surprise it must have been for them to arrive here instead! I'm told that they mostly stayed here, liking what they found in this country. The early Lebanese settlers were famous for their hawking of clothes and goods. Many of them covered the countryside on foot, selling their wares to country folk, and significant numbers of them ultimately settled in country towns, contributing to the prosperity of their communities.

My mother, Hannah, and my sisters, Alice and Paulette, arrived in Australia with my father in early 1925. After briefly visiting my grandparents in Sydney, they headed for the New South Wales country town of Werris Creek, and later moved to Cootamundra, where there seemed to be more opportunities for immigrants such as themselves with a tradition of shopkeeping and trading. After just a few months in the country, however, they returned to Sydney, where my father could practise as a chemist. They took up residence with my grandparents in a house on the corner of Walker and Redfern streets in the inner-city suburb of Redfern. The house fronted Walker Street, and adjoined the first Antioch Orthodox Church built in the Southern Hemisphere. The church had been constructed under my grandfather's supervision.

I was born on 15 November 1926, in a private hospital in the seaside suburb of Coogee. The building, on the corner of Coogee Bay and Carrington roads, is today a private residence. My debut as a sturdy 12-pounder (5.4 kilograms) apparently created a great stir. Dr Smith, who delivered me, quipped to my mother: 'We have a baby elephant!'

Alan Dalziel, a family friend who lived with his uncle, Jack Barbour, the local butcher whose shop was opposite our house in Redfern, owned a car, and he had driven my mother to the hospital. Alan, whom I later met on many occasions in the 1950s and 1960s, became private secretary to Dr Herbert Evatt, leader of the federal Labor opposition at the time, and, interestingly, featured prominently in the famous Petrov case. He was also an active member of the Temperance Society.

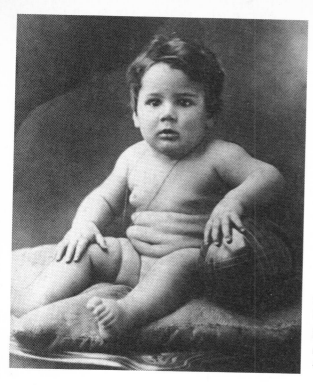

Appropriately with ball in hand, I am displaying a future frontrower's frame. The doctor who told my mother she had given birth to an 'elephant' wasn't kidding.

When I was five years old and my sisters were six and eight, my father opened a herbalist shop in George Street, Broadway (where the Carlton Brewery is now located), and for about a year we lived above the shop.

The suburb of Redfern is within sturdy walking distance of the Sydney city boundaries and was to be my home for many years. Cluttered with slums and the underprivileged, it truly lived up to its reputation as 'Struggle Town' during the poverty-stricken years of the Great Depression, and yet it had a soul and unique spirit, and a population of hardy folk who shared a warm kinship.

(Many years later, in 1947, when I was chosen at the age of twenty to tour the British Isles, France, Canada and the United States with the Australian rugby team, I experienced the pride

An early photograph of my mother, Hannah, sitting with me. My mother was the strength of our family, devoted to each and every one of us and a superb host to our friends. Visitors were never sent away from our Redfern house.

This family photograph was taken in Redfern more than seventy years ago. My mother stands at the centre, with my father at her right shoulder. I am being nursed by my grandmother (lower right), and my two older sisters, Alice and Paulette, sit on either side of my grandfather.

and loyalty that Redfern folk will show one of their own. The Redfern Town Hall was packed with people for my farewell function, during which I was presented with a kangaroo-skin rug. Two of my mentors from the Randwick Rugby Club — Wally Meagher and Len Palfreyman — were invited, and I was more than a little nervous. They were used to a more refined, less rough kind of environment in their home suburb of Coogee. The compere for the evening, Johnny Wade, a Redfern resident who worked as a singer at the Prince Edward Theatre in Sydney, was joined by Harry Willis and Glen Marks, who were also at the Prince Edward. When Johnny welcomed everyone, he announced that this was to be a fun night, 'So, would you all please leave your hardware [weapons] outside.' I thought that Wally and Len might faint!)

We moved to 88 Great Buckingham Street in Redfern in 1932, when I was six. My brother, George, was born in that house a couple of months after we moved in. During the Depression, Redfern was indeed a tough area and things were pretty desperate. People were hurting; there were no jobs and little food. However, there remained a fierce spirit. Everyone came together to help out with clothing and food. We youngsters helped Mr Jones, the local baker whose bakery was on Walker Street, distribute free bread to the needy. The queues were dishearteningly long.

I attended Cleveland Street Public School and, later, Crown Street Commercial School. Often I would arrive, like so many other impoverished youngsters from the area, barefooted, or wearing my father's hand-me-down shoes. Interestingly, one of my classmates,

Class 5B of Cleveland Street Public School, in Redfern, and that's me cradling our identification board. Most kids were barefooted — reflection of the battling families of the Redfern area at that time.

Kevin Lee, would eventually become my driver when I took up Town Hall duties as the deputy chief commissioner in 1987.

When my grandfather died in 1934, my father, who had qualified as a priest in Russia, took over his father's duties at the Antioch Orthodox Church. We moved into the house with my grandmother, next door to the church.

I seemed to be accident-prone in those growing-up years. Before I was ten years old I had been knocked down by bikes and a couple of cars. On one occasion, I unfurled an umbrella and leapt from the roof of our house in Great Buckingham Street in an attempt to fly. Predictably, I tumbled heavily to the ground below.

We made our own fun, playing cricket in the narrow streets and staging running races around the block. We became experts in scaling trams, jumping on and off them at high speed (sometimes backwards), and were never caught, despite the vigilance of the tram drivers and conductors. My friends and I would head out to Centennial Park where we would swim in one of the lakes that fronted on to Alison Road, opposite Randwick Racecourse. When a tram rattled by, we would leap out of the water naked and wave to the passengers.

I had some great schoolmates, including Joe Corey, who later became a professor of obstetrics and gynaecology in Hobart; Ron Saad, an eye specialist; Chika Dixon (affectionately known as 'Uncle Chika'), who is a prominent elder of the Aboriginal community and who once visited China with a former deputy prime minister; and Fred Solomon, who later worked with the United Nations in New York.

Our house, which had a long side wall, was directly opposite the Albert View Hotel in Redfern Street. Each Saturday, late in the afternoon, I would sit on the wall with my mates, waiting for the compulsory six o'clock closing of the hotel bar. From there we witnessed some terrific knock-'em-down, drag-'em-out fights among the local gladiators who were our heroes — Larry Gaffney, Tommy Colteau and Jack Riley, to name a few. All were renowned as tough street fighters.

Life in Redfern was a school of hard knocks. I was brought up in an environment where you had to fend for yourself. Looking back, having been reared in Redfern was the best education I could ever have had. It was a vibrant and colourful place. The strident cries of the hawkers roaming the streets selling rabbits, clothes props (used to hold up washing lines), ice, wood and coal were part of the Redfern culture.

Election day was always a big occasion. No one cared which party you voted for, as long as you voted for Bill McKell, and he happened to be the Labor candidate. Bill was loved and admired by everyone in Redfern. During church services at election time, my father would even instruct his parishioners to vote for Bill.

Bill and his family lived in Dowling Street, Redfern. He was a family friend, and many a time I was asked to run messages for him. I was privileged to meet him many times during his latter years, when he became premier and then governor-general. He was a man who made a great contribution to this country.

During the period my father served the church, I don't recall ever having a family meal at home with just ourselves at the table.

Our door was always open, and everyone, it seemed, was welcome. Our house was a general meeting place.

At school and in our neighbourhood I seemed to have been oblivious to social slurs and racism arising from our family being Lebanese. Though I was called 'Dago', 'Wog', 'Black Nick' and 'Midnight' by kids at school, I accepted it as fun. I could handle myself. Most boys of my age in Redfern had learned the hard way how to fight. My school lunch was always an object of great curiosity among the other children. Falafel, kibbeh and eggplant sandwiches certainly stood out from everyone else's pies or fish and chips.

Cricket was always my first love. If my friends and I weren't batting or bowling in the lanes of Redfern using a garbage bin as a wicket, we would be down at Redfern Park. I later played Green Shield cricket (under-sixteens) with the Waverley club. I wasn't very successful as a batsman; I was a more useful medium-pace bowler. Several of our team went on to play senior grade cricket, among them Kevin Featherstone and Mick Alterator. When I was a little older I played in the City and Suburban competition.

The Shehadies were mostly a religious family. My grandfather, my father and my uncle were all clergymen, but the tradition stopped with me. I'm a believer, but I could never imagine myself up there at the pulpit. However, I enjoy occasions such as Easter, which is a very important festival in the Orthodox Christian Church — coloured boiled eggs are distributed during the service, which is held late at night. It's a religious occasion and a time to reflect.

Each Sunday, my family was expected to attend the church service conducted by my father. I was an altar boy, along with several others. Stan Melick, who was older than the rest of us, endeavoured to organise the altar boys without much success. Jack Elias, Joe Corey and I were very naughty and played up something awful. No Sunday service went by without us having some sort of fight afterwards. Altar boys wore white gowns with blue stripes, which would finish up quite soiled from rolling in the dirt.

Our family was the centre of the local Lebanese community during my youth. Immigrants arriving in Australia would always go directly to the home of the local priest. We spoke a mixture of languages at home. The people arriving from Lebanon spoke Arabic, which I picked up and learned fairly well. We were friendly with many other Lebanese families — the Melicks, Scarfs, Abouds, Nassers, Coreys, Maloufs, Gazals and others, all good citizens who have made a notable contribution to this country.

The driving force in my family was undoubtedly my mother. While my father would probably win every argument, my mother would win every vote. My mother was the powerful one and I was in awe of her. She was a wonderful woman, and lived until the age of ninety-two. I can remember her being a heavy smoker until she was eighty, when she decided to give it up. She had a cigarette machine installed in the house in the early days, because you would get two packets free if you put in a machine. My mother loved a party. I could take ten, fifteen friends home at any time unannounced, and she would always produce food and drinks for them. She loved having people around.

My mother had great support, particularly from my older sister Alice, assisted by Paulette, who helped to run the household. George and Margaret, my youngest sister who was born in 1938, were too young to assist at the time. I was the rebel. I was never there. I was always out doing other things — mainly hanging around with my friends. I got away with not doing much around the house.

I have been greatly blessed with a caring, close-knit family, growing up during a period of economic and social hardship. I would not have been the person I have become if I had not been raised in this loving family during that unique time in history in that special part of Sydney. Later, what was really to shape my life was rugby football.

2 THE SPORTING LIFE

I left school at fourteen years of age because there was not enough money in the household to adequately support us all. I managed to get a job at Fox Movietone News as an assistant cameraman, but I was sacked after a month when I refused to wash the boss's car (I refused because it was raining). I then got a job at Ve-Toy Biscuits, a biscuit company situated in Young Street, Redfern, just around the corner from us. I was the office boy, but whenever someone went missing on the ovens, I would have to go and bake biscuits. The company was owned by the Tovey family. ('Ve-Toy' is an anagram of 'Tovey'.)

At the same time as I left school and found a job, a whole new world of rugby beckoned to me. Having divided my interest in sport between cricket and athletics up to that point, rugby football had played no part in my life. At the Combined High Schools Athletics Championships in my final year I had scooted around the Sydney Cricket Ground grass track for a second placing in the 800 yards event — my first venture out onto that famous turf. A few years later I would be out there again, this time facing the most intimidating sportsmen in the world, the New Zealand All Blacks rugby team. Exciting times lay ahead.

My good friend from school days, Colin Thornley, introduced me to the Coogee Surf Life Saving Club, but I wasn't yet sixteen, so I couldn't qualify for my bronze medallion. I used to stay with the Thornleys on most weekends, which was especially enjoyable because I loved to be near the water and Coogee Beach was just nearby. Colin's parents were a great influence on me. 'Pop' Thornley gave me lots of tips on the finer points of rugby, and 'Ma' Thornley was a great cook. They really made me feel welcome in their home; they were like my second parents. They had another son, Rex, who was serving in a commando unit in New Guinea (the front in the war against Japan had reached close to Australia's northern shores by that stage), and we looked up to him as something of a hero.

Most of the Coogee Surf Club members were associated with the Randwick Rugby Club, a club recognised far and wide as the 'Galloping Greens'. They wore myrtle-green jerseys and played an exhilarating game of high-speed handling and running rugby that

Lifesaving as a member of the Coogee Surf Club. This picture shows us in the traditional beach march-past preceding the many summer surf championship events. I am the beltman up front. Many footballers enjoyed off-season summer surf club activities, and competitors included the rugby league flyer Johnny Bliss, who was a beach sprint champion.

set the benchmark for Australian football. Great players came from Randwick's ranks, notably the legendary Cyril Towers, and Colin and Keith Windon, two highly mobile breakaways who would play during the war when on leave from the Services.

Still only fifteen when the football season came around, I went along to Coogee Oval with the Thornleys to join the Randwick Rugby Club. I knew little about rugby at the time, but I was reasonably fast and had good hands for a big lad, and was graded in the fourth-grade team as an inside centre. I took to the game very easily, being highly competitive, and gained much satisfaction from the strenuous training sessions.

I attended a gymnasium several times a week for extra fitness training. The gym, situated in Baptist Street in Redfern, was operated by a man named Dick Kerr. At times I sparred with Herb Narvo of boxing and Rugby League fame, and Jim Armstrong, another Rugby League celebrity and a popular Sydney Stadium pro wrestler at the time.

At one point, Dick Kerr was asked to supply some boxers from his gym to fight in a tournament at the Marrickville Army Barracks. I was one of those selected. On the night, I was introduced as 'Driver Shady' as I entered the ring. It was all a little frightening. I was pretty nervous, especially when I saw that my opponent was much older and bigger than I was — although I was big for my age. The referee was Joe Wallis, of Sydney Stadium fame. (Sydney Stadium, in the inner-city harbourside suburb of Rushcutters Bay, was the main boxing arena in Sydney in those days — all the championships were held there.)

The bell went. I had a very sharp and straight left hand, which landed a few telling punches. The bout was to be over four rounds and I received some quite heavy blows. At one point I was against the ropes and on the receiving end of some hefty blows, and all I could think of was not letting down my friends who were watching in the crowd.

When the final bell rang, I was crowned the winner on points and received a gold wristwatch. I couldn't get home fast enough to show it off to my parents, who had no idea where I had been. My father didn't mince his words, and I received a bigger belting from him than I had received in the ring.

My parents were totally opposed to any sport that might involve one being hurt. I didn't box again, although Dick Kerr believed that I had a bright future in boxing.

I had to work Saturday mornings at the biscuit factory. On one Saturday I said to the manager, Don Walker, 'Mr Walker, may I leave at eleven o'clock?' He asked me why, and I told him that I was playing fourth grade for the Randwick Rugby Club, and the game's kick-off was at midday. I hadn't realised that he was a fanatical rugby man who played for the Western Suburbs Rugby Club, and he cheerfully gave me the okay. He later became head of Millers Brewery and several other big organisations, and was always most helpful to me. He was to become a great friend and mentor.

One Saturday, soon after I joined the club, we were playing against Western Suburbs' fourth-grade team on a field outside Concord Oval when there was a hold-up, and some of the Randwick officials signalled to me to come off. A forward had been injured in the reserve-grade game next door on Concord Oval and I was to replace him. After I climbed the fence I was greeted by the team coach, Len Palfreyman, who said, 'You're just a youngster, but don't be overawed. You can do it. Just play your natural game.' I acquitted myself well enough to remain in reserve grade.

A few weeks later I had another astonishing promotion when the Randwick team played St George at Hurstville Oval. We had just finished our reserve-grade match when first-grader Jack Neary, the entrepreneur who was to bring the Beatles to Australia in the 1960s, was injured. Len Palfreyman told me I was to replace him. So, at the age of fifteen, I was making my first-grade debut in the role of a back-row forward. What an experience, playing alongside tough guys like Mal Murray, Bill Winter and Dave Isbister, and against St George's gnarled and legendary old ironman prop, Bill Cerutti. They were all about twice my age, but I remember how they still had enough wind to be free with their advice to the referee. There were many other tough characters in the Sydney rugby competition — players such as Perce Newton and Alby Stone of Eastern Suburbs, and Manly's Chad Paton, Alby Livingstone and Aub Hodgson.

RUGBY FLASHBACK

Sledging was part of rugby long before it became part of cricket. Perce Newton, the Eastern Suburbs stalwart in the Sydney competition, would lead his team out to line up against my club, Randwick. I would call out to him, 'Gee, your team is *ugly*.' He would reply, 'I'll give you ugly, you mug.' It's hard to believe that we were great mates.

My parents had no idea that I was playing rugby. They wouldn't have approved, so I didn't tell them. When I first started playing, I always left my rugby gear at the Thornleys' place. 'Pop' Thornley would look after it and would even clean my boots. It was simply that my father didn't understand sport. He was a scholar, and sport never interested him. It wasn't easy finding a way to participate in a sport that I had quickly come to love without upsetting my family.

By 1942 I was a regular first-grader, except when Keith Windon had Service leave and took my place. This was no disgrace to me, because Keith, Colin Windon's older brother, was a pre-war star, excelling against the South African Springboks when they toured Australia in 1937, but he had been denied the 1939 British Isles tour because of the outbreak of the Second World War. The Wallabies, Australia's national team, having already travelled to Britain, had the task of filling sandbags before they returned home without having kicked a football there.

In 1943 I moved into the second row, became a permanent first-grader and benefited from the team's great coach, Wally Meagher. Wally was a master exponent of the brand of running rugby that had brought the Randwick Club so much fame. In my opinion, he was even more knowledgeable in tactics than the legendary Cyril Towers. Wally had been a highly respected player in the 1920s and later became a respected administrator in the 1950s. During our Tuesday-night training sessions, without fear or favour he would pinpoint any mistakes we had made in the previous Saturday's game.

That year, still only sixteen years of age, I was selected in the Waratahs, the New South Wales team, to play the Combined Services as a back-row forward. Tom Pauling, Colin Windon, Max Carpenter and Don Furness turned out for the Services; and Mick Cremin, Rudy Cornelson, Arthur Buchan, Keith Little and Alby Stone played for the Waratahs.

By this time, my parents had become keen supporters of my rugby playing. They hadn't known anything about it until they

RUGBY FLASHBACK

It was the 1942 season and I had taken the field for Randwick against Parramatta at Coogee Oval. Looking up Hill Street, which runs down to the oval, I got a shock to see my father's car, a beige Dodge, parked on the hill. I guessed that he had read in the newspaper that I was playing in the game. Early in the second half, I had to leave the field with a gaping wound over my right eye. As I was escorted back to the grandstand, I looked up to see my father standing by the gates alongside our coach, Wally Meagher, and I expected the worst. But he said anxiously 'Will you be all right for next week?' So, he gave me the all-clear for my footy career.

From then on, my father came to watch every match, and my sisters became involved in organising tea for the players after each game. In fact, my father became so keen that he followed us around New Zealand in 1949 to watch the games. New Zealand at that time was part of his parish as a clergyman, and whenever we sighted him he was surrounded by people. Our hooker, Don Furness, would say: 'There he is. Loved by all.' And that's how the team always referred to him.

My mother also became a fervent supporter. Years later, in the 1954 Test against Fiji at the Sydney Cricket Ground when I was captain for the first time in Australia, some fans in the grandstand started calling out that I was a 'mug'. Mum promptly clouted one of them with her umbrella!

started seeing my name in the papers. Previously completely unaware of any kind of sport, my father became such a rugby fan that he would refuse to perform marriage ceremonies on Saturdays in winter because it was the football season!

In 1944 I again played for New South Wales against the Armed Services; however, I missed out on selection to the team in 1945.

In 1946 I was chosen to visit Queensland with the New South Wales team as a utility forward. On this trip, my first out of the state, we travelled by train, and I was naive enough to fall for a prank the team manager and coach played on me. Clyde Kennedy (later Sir Clyde and chairman of the Sydney Turf Club) was the manager and a former international forward. Wylie Breckenridge was the coach. They assured me that if I kept my eyes open, I would see wild buffalo from the train. Alas, my vigil continued late into the evening, without any sightings. I felt a bit of a fool afterwards, but I put it down to growing up in the rugby fraternity, and my excitement about the tour soon overrode any feelings of embarrassment.

Ron Rankin, the distinguished Australian Air Force pilot, was our captain and my room-mate. The team included Trevor Allan, Eric Tweedale, Phil Hardcastle, Arthur Buchan, Cyril Burke, Max Howell, Terry MacBride and Charlie Eastes who, in 1947–48, would also be my team-mates on the fabulous Wallaby tour to the British Isles, France and North America.

I played the preliminary match at Toowoomba, but wasn't selected for the interstate game against the Queensland team, which was captained by Bill McLean. Later, I was omitted from the

Australian team, also captained by McLean, which was announced to tour New Zealand on the first post-war trip. (Bill was also to lead the Wallabies on our 1947–48 tour to Europe and North America.) I was nineteen years of age. I still had a lot to learn and a long way to go.

3 GETTING SERIOUS ABOUT THE GAME

In 1946 I was working in the biscuit factory and playing regular first-grade rugby with Randwick and New South Wales, but my parents were convinced I needed a trade that would stand me in good stead in later life. I had three uncles living in Bathurst, just over the Dividing Range west of Sydney, who operated a successful dry-cleaning business. The idea of living and working in Bathurst didn't appeal to me very much — and I certainly didn't want to play rugby in Bathurst. The Wallaby tour to New Zealand was coming up, followed by the 1947 tour to the United Kingdom, and I believed I had more of a chance of tour selection if I was

In action with the Galloping Greens. In this scene from a Coogee Oval encounter with traditional rivals **Gordon** in the Sydney club premiership competition, I am making a bullocking run.

playing under the eyes of the selectors in the Sydney competition with the Randwick club. However, this was to be my opportunity to learn a trade, and I felt I had to take it. I didn't want to let my parents down.

I said goodbye to my beloved Redfern and moved to Bathurst, where I became a boarder at Mrs Cobby's Metropolitan Hotel. My duties in my uncles' factory included feeding the clothes into machines, spotting stains and preparing the clothes for pressing.

Most nights I trained alone, even in mid-winter, by running to Kelso and back — a distance of 6 or 7 kilometres. Occasionally, I would go along to the local oval and have some sprint training on the grass with one of the local Bathurst Rugby League teams. John O'Toole, who later became Country League president, was very helpful to me.

Each Friday night I would catch the midnight train to Sydney, which arrived at Central Station at 6 a.m., allowing me a few hours' sleep before my game began. If I finished my work in the cleaning room early on the Friday, I would get out on the Sydney road and hitch a ride instead of catching the late train. I would return to Bathurst on Sunday evening on the *Western Mail* train at 9.30 p.m., in what was known as the 'dog box' carriage, with foot-warmers on the floor. I would arrive in Bathurst at 3 a.m. and it always seemed to be freezing cold.

During the summer months I played the odd game of cricket with one of the local clubs, but, on the whole, I didn't mix much with other people and was quite lonely. Occasionally my Uncle John, who wasn't married, would accompany me to country dances

---

RUGBY FLASHBACK

In the early days I had to drop out of the Randwick team for the club match against Eastwood, and my replacement was Reg Perry. It happened that Reg and I looked a little alike. Joe Newsome, the rugged Eastwood forward and skipper, welcomed Reg with a whack between the eyes, saying, 'Shehadie, I've waited a couple of seasons to do that.' Reg was as tough as teak, and by the end of the game Joe Newsome had come off second best.

---

at places such as Blayney and Trunkey Creek. But I mostly kept to myself.

Despite all my training efforts and travelling to Sydney for matches, I wasn't selected in the team to tour New Zealand that year. Although I was disappointed, I didn't give up.

The New Zealand All Blacks came to Australia in the winter of 1947. How massive and tough they were, and how hard they played the game! They stayed at the Coogee Bay Hotel in Coogee and, with a Saturday off, they sauntered down to the nearby Coogee Oval to watch Randwick play Gordon in a club premiership match. The two clubs were at full strength and turned on a pretty torrid encounter. I felt I had a good game, and evidently impressed the New Zealand manager, Norman McKenzie, the doyen of All Blacks football, who took it upon himself to walk across to the Australian selectors present and praise my potential as an up-and-coming prospect. The outcome of this unexpected support saw me instantly added to the New South Wales squad that had been announced earlier. I have always felt indebted to Norman McKenzie for giving me that critical break.

I played for the New South Wales B team against the New Zealanders — my first physical encounter with the granite men from the Shaky Isles. I failed to make the Australian team for the first Test, in which we were beaten 13–5, in Brisbane, but I was at home in Redfern the next day when the telephone rang and a reporter from the Sydney *Daily Mirror*, Ken Archer, told me I had been selected in the second Test side. I refused to believe him, but then my team-mate Trevor Allan rang to confirm it. Chosen in the second row, I was to play for Australia before my home crowd on the sacred Sydney Cricket Ground (SCG). I had to pinch myself to believe it.

I was still working and living in Bathurst, but I stayed with my parents in Redfern during the week prior to that match. The team was to assemble on the Tuesday. I was so pumped up that, on the Monday, I went for a run from my Redfern home up Driver Avenue to the SCG, just to get a preview of the atmosphere that would mark the big occasion ahead. When I returned home from the run, I opened a tin of sardines and in the process sliced my finger open. In a panic, I rang Dr Alex Moir, my mother's doctor and a great family friend, who came around to stitch the wound. Nothing was going to stop me from playing. Concerned that the injury could jeopardise my medical examination, which would determine whether I was fit to play the match, I disguised it by strapping both my hands. The stitches broke, but I passed the examination.

The big day arrived and I was jumping out of my skin with the excitement of playing in my first Test. My parents, sisters and brother were all there to watch the game. I remember walking into the home-team dressing room, situated at the southern end of the Members' Stand, and picking up my number 11 jersey, shorts and socks. I then moved quietly off into a corner to change. Big, genial Queensland prop Bob McMaster was relaxed, laughing and joking, but I was more concerned with saying a few prayers.

When the time came to take the field, we lined up in front of the Members' Stand. The All Blacks' captain, Fred Allen, then led out these huge New Zealanders, who lined up in front of us. I had never even *watched* a rugby Test before, and there I was, *playing* in one! The All Blacks carried a huge reputation, perhaps sharing world champion honours with their great rivals, the South African Springboks. Most of the All Blacks came out of the Kiwi team who had played a number of games in Britain at the end of the war, notably Bob Scott, Wally Argus, Johnny Simpson, Has Catley, Ray Dalton, J.B. Smith, Neville Thornton and, of course, the skipper, Fred Allen himself. Wow!

They kicked off and the ball came straight to me. I caught it, and, probably out of sheer fright, made a dash down the centre for about 10 metres. I was pumped — I could have run all day. We gave the All Blacks a scare in that game, trailing only 8–11 at half-time. Bob Scott's uncanny ability to pilot home goals from a long range decided the outcome, and veteran critics enthusiastically compared his full-back play to that of the legendary George Nepia of the 1920s. And as if Scott's penalties weren't enough, skipper Fred Allen surprised the 30 000-strong crowd by tossing the ball to the big loose forward, Neville Thornton, for a penalty attempt — from way out — and he booted the ball clean through the goal posts. It was a very tight game, although we ended up losing 14–27.

4 FIRST WALLABIES
INTERNATIONAL TOUR, 1947–48

About twelve months after I started doing the Bathurst–Sydney trek on weekends, the 1947–48 Wallaby touring team was about to be announced, the prize a wonderful nine-month tour through the British Isles, France, the United States and Canada. It was the trip of a lifetime, and I was in the running.

The team was to be announced at 2 p.m. on ABC radio on the Monday. We had played the All Blacks at the SCG on the Saturday, and the next day, together with my Randwick Club mates Mick Cremin and Don Furness, I went to the Coogee Bay Hotel to bid the New Zealanders farewell after their successful tour of Australia.

Sir Leslie Herron, the president of the Australian Rugby Union, and Johnny Wallace, the chairman of selectors, walked by us, and Sir Leslie asked me if I would drive Johnny to his city hotel if he couldn't get a cab. Cremin and Furness urged me to ask him during the car trip whether we would be surfing in Sydney during the summer ahead. If he said 'yes', it would mean we hadn't been selected for the tour. Johnny Wallace got his cab, but Sir Leslie said to me quietly: 'I asked you because you know London's traffic rules — and if you don't, then you should learn them.' It was an encouraging tip-off, to say the least.

I was so nervous on the day of the announcement that I locked myself in the back room of our home in Redfern to listen to the radio alone. The names of the four second-rowers were read out, and I wasn't among them. Disaster! But then came the twenty-fourth selection of the thirty-man tour party: utility forward, Nick Shehadie. What a relief! My parents, late converts to rugby and sport, were thrilled at my selection. Within minutes our house was packed with well-wishers, and amid the high excitement I felt I might collapse. Mr Smirl, the proprietor of the Albert View Hotel, sent over some beer. Jack, the butcher, arrived. No one could be heard over the din. I thought, 'You beaut! Goodbye, Bathurst!'

The touring side was brimful of experienced players, some of whom had seen service in the war that had just ended. At twenty years old, I was the second-youngest (Keith Winning, the Queensland breakaway, was the youngest).

I had to return to Bathurst to pack my things for the nine-month tour. Prior to leaving for the tour I was given a wonderful reception

The 1947–48 Wallaby touring team, which attained one of the all-time great achievements by not having its goal line crossed in the four internationals against Ireland, Wales, Scotland and England. The Wallabies won twenty-nine of their thirty-five tour games, scoring ninety-eight tries and conceding only twenty-four.

by the people of that town, hosted by my uncles in the local Church of England hall.

Right through my teenage years I had been too busy training, playing sport or working, to think about girls. I was also very nervous around the opposite sex. By this time I had already met Marie Bashir, who would later become my wife, but there was no indication at the time that anything would develop between us, nor that she would become a permanent part of my life. Our families knew each other through the local Lebanese community, where the priest's home was always at the centre of things. Marie's grandmother, who was known to everyone as 'Grandma Melick', lived not far from us in Elizabeth Street, Redfern, next to the clothing warehouse that was owned and operated by Marie's extended family.

Before I left on my tour, my father said, 'I want you to go around and say goodbye to Grandma Melick, because she may not be alive when you get back.' (She would have been aged in her seventies at the time.) Marie's grandmother and my father were good friends. Alert and intelligent, she lived until the age of 105, and attended our wedding.

Marie, a schoolgirl of about sixteen at the time of my departure with the Wallabies, was in her final year at Sydney Girls' High School. Her parents lived in Narrandera in the state's central south-west, and she was staying with her grandmother so that she could attend high school in Sydney. Her mother was an old girl from Sydney Girls', where Marie's sister Helen also attended.

Being the big, tough footballer, I asked Marie, 'What would you like me to bring you back from Paris?'

She laughingly replied, 'A painting from the Left Bank of the Seine.' To be honest, I didn't know the Left Bank from the Right Bank, and I never gave it another thought. All I could think about was the tour.

In July 1947 the day finally came to sail out of Sydney Harbour on the passenger liner *Orion*. We left from No. 7 wharf in Woolloomooloo in Sydney, and thousands of people were there to farewell the team — the first Australian sporting side to visit the United Kingdom after the war. I took with me a cabin trunk and two suitcases, and my cabin-mate for six weeks, Bob McMaster, arrived, I am sure, with only an overnight bag. It was quite an experience rooming with 'Wallaby' Bob, as he was affectionately known. He would come in some evenings after a drink or two and promptly put a hefty headlock on me, calling me 'Midnight', and I would end up being thrown against the wall. It was all in good fun! A friend of my father's, Canon Hammond, the rector of St Philips Church in Sydney, who was making a visit to England, occupied the cabin next to us. I had to apologise for the noise and tell him that Bob was just out of the army and suffering from war nerves.

Many prominent people were on the ship, including the great singer Peter Dawson; the comedian Dick Bentley; the aviator Jimmy Mollison; Sir Leslie Morsehead, head of the Orient company, and Lady Morsehead; and Diana Hart, a dancer who, some years earlier, had been badly burned in the dreadful Tivoli Theatre fire in Sydney. I became good friends with Diana, who was aged in her late twenties. I would take her swimming in the ship's pool at night — to protect her privacy. I was much younger than she; I was like her

My proud mother farewells me on the deck of the *Orion* in 1947, just before our departure for the momentous tour of the British Isles and France. 'Have a wonderful time,' she wished me on my first tour venture, and I certainly did.

little brother. I used to sit with her and talk with her. She was very attractive. I'm sure that she had a big crush on my team-mate Wal Dawson, who was closer to her in age.

Not having been to sea before — in fact, not having been any-where outside New South Wales besides Queensland before — it was all a thrill for me.

We had a scrummaging machine (a machine that substitutes for an opposition pack of forwards) onboard, and each morning except Sundays, after hot Bonox and a piece of toast, we were up on deck at six o'clock really doing it tough. We were extremely fit and joined in all the physical sports — especially swimming in the ship's pool.

On leaving Fremantle after crossing the Great Australian Bight, the voyage really moved into top gear for us. After a long stint at sea, we arrived at our first overseas port, Colombo, in Ceylon (now Sri Lanka), where we were entertained by the Australian trade commissioner and the local rugby enthusiasts, who were mainly expatriates. The dinner held for us at the famous Galle Face Hotel

Relaxing on deck with my team-mates. From left: Arthur Buchan, me, Wallaby Bob and Brian Piper.

was certainly a night to remember. I was seated between Bob McMaster and Mick Cremin when Mick suggested that the musicians, who were playing 'My Blue Heaven', should instead be playing 'McNamara's Band'. I couldn't stop 'Wallaby' Bob from marching over to the band leader, who ignored his request. Bob wasn't going to be ignored, so he seized the microphone and sang 'My Blue Heaven' beautifully. Arnold Tancred, the manager, chastised me for not controlling the pair, but Mohammed Ali wouldn't have been able to control them, let alone me!

Swimming pool activities aboard the *Orion*. I have my back to the camera, and Brian Piper (left) and Bill McLean stand on either side of me.

Aden, in Yemen, was our next port of call, then Egypt's Port Said, where we berthed in the early hours of the morning. I awoke to the sounds of the local police banging on my cabin door to tell me that my aunt, my mother's sister whom I had never met, had flown down from Lebanon to see me. Bob McMaster held the police at bay — suspicious, perhaps, that I was about to be kidnapped. Well, my aunt, an English teacher, proved to be a wonderful, warm woman who looked very much like my mother. We spent a great day together.

Finally, we arrived in England. The white cliffs of Dover looked awesome. Upon our arrival at Tilbury we were met with a warm welcome by members of the rugby hierarchy. Our team looked suntanned, fit and very smart — we were all wearing suits.

After six weeks of shipboard life, it was great to be on firm ground again. The coach journey into London took several hours, and the devastation of the buildings after the wartime German bombing raids was distressing to see, more so for some members of our team, such as Eddie Broad, Ken Kearney and Neville Emery, who had been in Britain on service with the RAAF, and for whom the trip was reviving unhappy memories.

We stayed at the Park Lane Hotel, which was to become our London home many times during the tour. Seeing Buckingham Palace, Trafalgar Square and all the action in Piccadilly Circus for the first time, I was awestruck by the history and sheer scale of this famous city.

After two days of sightseeing, we left by train for Penzance in Cornwall, where we were to stay for three weeks for our pre-tour training and preparation. The people of Penzance adopted the team with great warmth, and we made some lasting friendships. Food rationing was still operating and the local farmers would bring us fresh eggs and poultry. Meat was at a premium. The late autumn days were superb and warm, and we trained every day except Sunday, from 9 a.m. until noon. Bill McLean, our tour captain, was a hard taskmaster and never let up on us. Indeed, the training was much harder than playing a match.

After training we would go swimming or sailing in the harbour with the locals. The Marine Hotel, where we stayed, was pleasant and nicely situated on the picturesque waterfront. I shared a room with Arthur Buchan and Eric Tweedale, who were like fathers to me, teaching me a good deal about life.

RUGBY FLASHBACK

In 1947 the Wallabies had beaten Abertillery and Cross Keys. At the dinner that evening, the club president was making his speech and telling the gathering that losing didn't matter, because it was only a game. A voice from the back called out, 'Well, why did you keep the bloody score?'

On one occasion we called into the local pub and a man approached us, saying he had met many Australians during the war. We thought, here we go again: 'Do you know Bill Smith from Sydney?' But we were surprised when he asked if we knew Ron Rankin.

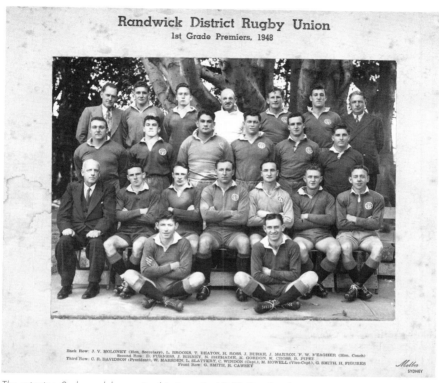

Randwick District Rugby Union
1st Grade Premiers, 1948

Back Row: J. V. MOLONEY (Hon. Secretary), L. BROOKS, T. BEATON, H. ROSS, J. BURKE, J. MARRON, F. W. M'EAGHER (Hon. Coach)
Second Row: D. FURNESS, J. BIRNEY, N. SHEHADIE, K. GORDON, K. CROSS, R. PIPER
Third Row: C. R. DAVIDSON (President), W. MARSDEN, L. SLATTERY, C. WINDON (Capt.), M. HOWELL (Vice-Capt.), G. SMITH, H. FIGURES
Front Row: G. SMITH, R. CAWSEY

Mellon
SYDNEY

The winning Sydney club premiership team in 1948, Randwick.

The 1949 Wallabies, winners of the Bledisloe Cup in New Zealand that year.

Going in to assist a team-mate against South Africa in a Test in 1953.

Action on the field — a provincial match in South Africa in 1953.

RIGHT *Chatting with the famous Welsh rugby writer JBG Thomas (centre) and Wallaby coach Bob Templeton in Cardiff in 1981, during my time as manager of the Wallabies.*

BELOW *With two famous goalkickers of the 1940s, Bob Scott of New Zealand (centre) and Okey Geffin of South Africa.*

The Western Mail

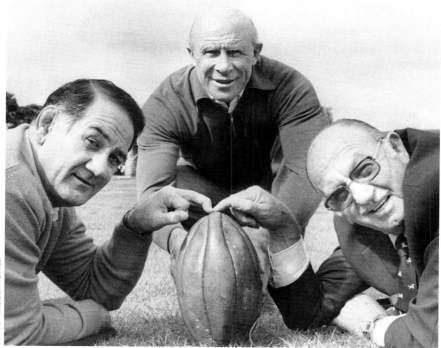

Merv Griffiths, / Dominion Post

LEFT *Nursing Prince William of Gloucester at St James's Palace, London, during the 1947–48 Wallabies tour of the United Kingdom.*

BELOW *At Government House in 1971, on being invested with an Order of the British Empire, with my wife Marie and my mother.*

On the occasion of being invested with an Order of the British Empire by the then governor of New South Wales, Sir Roden Cutler.

I was created a Knight Bachelor in 1976. The honour was bestowed upon me by the then governor-general, Sir John Kerr, at Government House.

A visit by the then prime minister Gough Whitlam to the Sydney Town Hall during my time as lord mayor.

Reuniting with old friend Charlie Watts, drummer of the Rolling Stones, and his wife Shirley, prior to a performance at the SCG. With us is my daughter Alexandra.

ABOVE *With my successor as chairman of the SCG Trust, Rodney Cavalier, standing in front of the famous SCG Members' Stand.*

TOP RIGHT *I was honoured to have a stand at the Sydney Football Stadium (now called Aussie Stadium) named after me in 1999.*

BELOW *My son, Michael, and his wife Jane, with Nicholas and Victoria at a family wedding.*

LEFT *Carrying the Olympic torch in Ballina, New South Wales, in 2000.*

BELOW *With my daughters, Alexandra (left) and Susan.*

In an incredible coincidence, Ron, who was a distinguished flyer during the Second World War, was also a rugby international and a former player with my club, Randwick. We were invited to this man's farm at Land's End for supper, which led to my spending many happy times with his family, and especially his daughters, Ann and Mary, who were a year or two younger than me. We had a lot in common, and I hit it off with Ann. Whenever any dances were held, I took Ann as my partner. I also found a second home with Dick Chappell and his wife, Edith, who lived nearby in Newlyn. I had met them at a civic reception organised by the Borough of Penzance. I still keep in contact with their son, Derek, and many years later, when I was 'surprised' on Channel Nine's 'This is Your Life' television program, I was thrilled to find that Edith Chappell had been flown out from England to join me on the stage. I still correspond with Ann and the Chappells — we have remained friends.

At the end of our tour we presented 'Wally the Wallaby', our mascot (stuffed, of course), to the Penzance Rugby Club, and he is still there in a glass case. Years later, as lord mayor of Sydney, I presented a plaque of the city of Sydney to the Borough of Penzance.

I was selected to play in the first tour match against Combined Devon and Cornwall at Cambourn. It was the first time I had encountered a team playing with identifying letters on their backs, instead of numbers. I found it very strange. We had plenty of support; indeed, I felt that the township of Penzance was on our side. We won quite comfortably, with Charlie Eastes, the speedy and sturdy Manly winger, scoring two exciting tries, but naturally enough our team was a little short of match practice.

There were tears when we left Penzance for Birmingham. Wonderful friendships had been made, and the railway station was lined with our new friends while a local band played 'Auld Lang Syne'. That sojourn in Cornwall was a superb way to start what was to be a memorable tour. We played forty-one matches all told — thirty in the United Kingdom and Ireland, winning twenty-five; then ten matches in France, winning nine; and finally, six matches in the United States and Canada. The absolute highlight, of course, was the Wallabies' proud record of not having a try scored against us in any one of the four international matches against the Home teams — Scotland, Ireland, England and Wales.

Unfortunately, though, the team sustained two very serious injuries, losing our captain, Bill McLean, in only the sixth game — against the Combined Services at Twickenham. There was irony in this. Bill had arrived in Britain with the 1939 Wallabies, only for their tour to be abandoned when the war broke out. McLean's 1939 Wallabies had arrived amid international tension. Their liner, *Mooltan*, was diverted to Devon, where they moved into a Torquay hotel. Britain declared war against Germany on the following day, so the players occupied their days filling sandbags, helping to evacuate children to country towns, and visiting the famous turf at Twickenham, where they were photographed wearing gasmasks. The return voyage to Australia must have been hazardous, the ship zigzagging a course so as to avoid German submarines. A match was hastily arranged in Bombay so that those players who had never played for Australia could pull on the jersey.

Tour tragedy — the broken leg suffered by Wallaby skipper Bill McLean, playing against the Combined Services at Twickenham. It meant a premature end to the tour for the rugged Queenslander, who did not play rugby again. Being duty boy for the day, I am helping our captain dismount from a coach in this picture, with encouragement from Arthur Buchan and Eric Davis.

Bill McLean's tragic injury came late in the Services game at Twickenham. He was caught in a ruck, and the 'crack' of his leg breaking resounded across the giant stands. We had fielded three of our doctors in our team that day — Phil Hardcastle, Doug Keller and Clem Windsor — so they were on the spot to tend and console the skipper.

Our match against the top Welsh side, Newport, cost us our champion winger, Charlie Eastes, who broke his arm. Neither McLean nor Eastes played again on the tour, so, at the tender age of twenty, Trevor Allan took over leadership of the Wallabies and performed a remarkable job. In those days, injured players could not be replaced from home or on the day.

The tour manager, Arnold Tancred, was a very strict disciplinarian who was determined that we would win as many matches as possible. He would constantly remind us that we would only be remembered for the number of matches we won. He didn't endear himself to many with his approach. Jack Pollard, in his book *The Game and the Players*, made this comment: 'The only criticism of Tancred was that he relied perhaps too heavily on the team's proven stars, and did not give newcomers many opportunities. He barred sports writers travelling with the team from staying in the same hotel, was uncooperative with the Press, and the team did not enjoy very sympathetic media coverage.'

For a young man like me, seeing the world for the first time, each day was an adventure. I didn't have a care in the world. In the Adelphi Hotel in Liverpool, some of us were travelling in a lift to our rooms when Arch Winning said to a woman sharing the lift, 'You look like Mae West.'

'I am, honey. Come up and see me some time,' she said. And she was.

The hospitality everywhere was outstanding. Our daily out-of-pocket stipend was just five shillings — enough to buy toothpaste and the odd drink — yet we could hardly spend it. Today the players receive hundreds of thousands of dollars, and some still think they are worth more. In my day, players would walk across hot coals to represent their country.

While we won our first few games comfortably, the dark cloud looming ahead of us was Cardiff, the pride of Welsh rugby. 'Wait until you get to Cardiff,' was the cry we heard repeatedly. The Welsh, we found, were rugby fanatics, and Cardiff was certainly a magnificent team, full of big, tough players, and quick, too. If this wasn't intimidating enough, we stepped out onto the Welsh ground to mass singing by the crowd, and it was singing done with passion, meant to inspire the home team. There was no question as to who they wanted to win.

The Cardiff match was tough and rough, and we lost our hooker, Wal Dawson, with torn ligaments in the rib cage, and me with a dislocated shoulder. Although we didn't leave the field, we were passengers for the rest of the game. We lost — our first tour game defeat in the five games played so far — at the hands of players that included Bleddyn Williams, Dr Jack Mathews, Haydn Tanner, Ben Tamplin and Bill Cleaver, who were all to become greats of Welsh rugby.

I am still good mates with Jack Mathews and Bleddyn Williams. When I visited the Cardiff Rugby Club recently, I met up with the good doctor and asked him if, at eighty-one, he still practised medicine. He replied that he did, but that he only had one patient, and that was Bleddyn Williams — they would meet every Tuesday in the Cardiff club. Then they took me on a tour of the club. I was thrilled to see my old Australian jersey in a glass case. There is also an Australian jersey of mine in the Trophy Room at Twickenham.

Our match in the tin-mining town of Llanelly, deep in the Welsh valleys, was one I'm never likely to forget, even if I didn't play in the game. Llanelly had beaten the 1908 Wallabies and had adopted a song about how they had triumphed. They conveniently couldn't remember the game they had lost to the Waratahs in 1927.

The rough stuff was on from the very first whistle. Arthur Buchan was tackled on the sideline, pushed into the crowd and punched several times. Graeme Cooke was cautioned by the local referee for rough play, then Colin Windon was ordered from the field — seemingly for doing nothing. With that, all hell broke loose, with our manager, Arnold Tancred, stepping out onto the field and calling our team to come off. They didn't. The crowd was jeering Colin as he left, the band played, and there was some spitting on poor Colin. Bob McMaster followed Arnold to protect him and assist him from the field. The match restarted with our ranks a man short and facing problems with a very biased referee. We won in the dying minutes of the game.

The dinner that evening saw the locals sitting on one side of the hall and ourselves on the other. The speeches were short and sharp and we left without fraternising. As we boarded our coach to return to our hotel in Swansea, the streets were crowded and there was much booing. 'Wallaby Bob' McMaster leaned out of the bus window and yelled to the mob, 'We beat you bastards!' Colin Windon was to suffer a two-match suspension because the Irish delegate designated to hear the case was unavailable for the first week of the inquiry. The rules dictated — and still do today — that a player cannot take part in a match until the disciplinary committee has met and heard the case.

Ten years later, during the 1957 Wallaby tour, I returned to Llanelly the night before our scheduled match, accompanied by the journalist Phil Tresidder, who had been with us on that earlier tour. We met many of the players who had played in that infamous game.

It's marvellous what time can achieve, especially with a few beers. All was made up!

Later in the tour we visited the House of Commons and the House of Lords in London, which was a great experience, but to top it all off we subsequently visited 10 Downing Street, where the prime minister, Clement Attlee, received us. He gave us a wonderful tour of the building, identifying photographs and providing some history. In his writing room I'm sure he had laid out on purpose, within easy reach, his personal writing paper with '10 Downing Street' displayed on the letterhead — which we enthusiastically souvenired. We were writing home on the prime minister's notepaper for weeks afterwards. Indeed, Trevor Allan still has some of it.

We also visited St James Palace, where the Duke of Gloucester (at one time the governor-general of Australia) gave us a reception. His young son, Prince William, jumped on my back and we had our photograph taken.

The absolute highlight of our tour was the visit to Buckingham Palace, a day we will all always remember. Arriving on a beautiful winter's morning, our coach drove us through the huge iron gates, where we were met and escorted inside the palace by the palace staff. Once inside, we formed a half-circle. King George VI and the Queen greeted us. Bill McLean escorted His Majesty to the reception area, and Arnold Tancred escorted the Queen, but all eyes were on Princess Margaret, escorted by Trevor Allan. Jeff Noseda, the team secretary, accompanied Princess Elizabeth. The Royals had a word to say to each one of us, and we had an anxious moment, keeping our fingers crossed, when His Majesty met Phil Hardcastle, as both suffered from a speech impediment. Luckily, all went well.

The British hospitality continued, with the Australian actor, John McCallum, who was a schoolmate of Bill McLean, inviting the team to Ealing Studios to watch him making a film. We were taken onto the sets and were most impressed, particularly with Greta Gynt, who was performing with John.

In Ireland, the president, Eamonn de Valera, entertained the team at a cocktail party. While many dignitaries were present, we were only interested in Captain de Groot, the celebrated figure who, twenty-five years earlier, rode his horse onto Sydney Harbour Bridge and cut the ribbon before the premier, Jack Lang, could officially open the bridge. The iconic status of De Groot, then living in Ireland, certainly made a great impression on us.

So much for the social side. The tour was long and hard. We played matches each Wednesday and Saturday, and not always in favourable weather or with adequate ground conditions.

Having watched the three earlier Tests against Ireland, Scotland and Wales from the bench, after a series of strong games I forced my way into the team for the Test against England at Twickenham, the last of the four Home internationals and a crucial one for us. Having beaten Ireland and Scotland and losing through two penalty goals against Wales, we were determined not to have a try recorded against us in a Test. Prior to the match, which was on 3 January 1948, we had several days preparation at Eastbourne, on the English south coast, amid the New Year celebrations. But for the chosen fifteen, celebrations were decidedly subdued. We were really focused.

The third of January was a lovely day in London, and the sight of the huge grandstands filling up with thousands of spectators was a sight to behold. A great number of Cornish people came to support us. Our dressing room was almost silent, every player well aware that the job ahead of us wasn't going to be easy. I was to play loose head prop, Ken Kearney hooker and Eric Tweedale tight head. Alan Walker, now a dual international cricketer–footballer, was included in the centres to play alongside Trevor Allan.

My job in the lineouts was to follow 'Jika' Travers, the Australian-born Oxford scholar who was vice-captain of the England side. We bumped heavily in the very first lineout and he delivered a hefty elbow that left me with a swollen cheek. Our second-rowers Graeme Cooke and Don (Joe) Kraefft dominated the lineouts and we were winning more than our share of the set scrums three to one. The game was fast and furious, and suddenly our goal line was threatened with the English winger, Swarbrick, in open country and flying for the line for the try that would destroy our dream of maintaining an unbroken try line through the Tests. Here is a graphic description of what followed, from the pen of the English rugby writer Denzel Batchelor, author of the book *Days Without Sunset*:

Swarbrick licked up the pass like a sprinter head down for the finish. Sheer pace carried him on. Tonkin could not get to him. He swerved out, his flying feet not brushing the chalk from the touch line. Piper's dash to the corner was too late. Swarbrick pounced forward — he was clear! The 70 000 crowd were on their toes. Wild arms waved to high heaven. The Twickenham Valley, pinched between the canyon grandstands, reverberated with thundering clanging to a crescendo. He was not only clear — he was through! He was indeed over the line, safely, marvellously home. He had but to fall on his face and England would be a try up. A dead man must have scored us three points. And then, as Swarbrick hurled himself down, a pinpointed rocket caught him, swept him through mid-air, ball and all, into the no-man's-land of touch in goal. Have you ever seen this sight? The whirling into touch, by side-on tackle, of the wing three-quarter who has crossed the goal line. You have never seen rugby at its most thrilling unless you have. No mere scoring of a try can compare with it. Nothing else in the whole game can offer such a split-second quintessence of drama.

What a wordsmith was Batchelor, and how can such a physically brutal game as rugby deserve such eloquence? The magic tackler, of course, was Trevor Allan — who else?

I chuckled as I read Batchelor's account of the South African-born English full-back, Sidney Newman, kicking for a penalty goal that would keep England in the match.

Calmly, slowly, he measured the angle, stood there silent, pondering the wind that blew against England and eddied in the canyon between the grandstands. He did his mental arithmetic — he made his calculations. Then the ball was down. A few steps of gentle trot and the great kick soared. The thunder-cheer of all

Twickenham upsoared with it. There went a goal, star-destined and clear-cut every inch of the way from the toe of goal post Sidney Newman's size-ten boot. And at the last moment came a little gust of wind which had surely started in childhood as a southerly buster roaring from Manly over the city of Sydney, which had travelled north, faster than by British Airways, out-flanking the desert sand storms and the sirocco, the mistral and the Channel gales. It had come at last to Twickenham, just in time to puff its interfering and detestable way aslant the ground, to drag Newman's great kick out of its grandly ruled straight line, to swing out and round to hit a goal post, and drop pointless, into play.

That day, Alan Walker chip-kicked ahead, regathered the ball with the skill of a slips fieldsman, and touched down for a glorious try. Then the mighty Colin Windon tormented the English captain and five-eighth, Tom Kemp, one more time, the ball rolling loose, and Windon pouncing to set off on a zigzagging run from half-way for his second try. Only the genius of Colin Windon could have scored that try. What a party there was that night to celebrate both our win at Twickenham and the achievement of maintaining our unbreached goal line!

Batchelor wrote that, while the Australian attitude to sport is dour, grim and puritanical when approaching all games from archery to zebra racing, they relax into light-heartedness and schoolboy zest when they pull on their boots for rugby football. The first of two influencing factors was the vision and example set by that philosopher, Johnny Wallace of Oxford and Waratah fame. The former Rhodes scholar and Wallaby captain led the Waratah team of 1927, famous for their new brand of open, fast rugby. The second influencing factor was the need to compete with the fast-moving Rugby League code, its neighbour down-under. Sportsmen in England could be too content to be 'honourable' losers, Batchelor wrote. He pointed out how the Paris press had, that winter, celebrated France's defeat of England in Paris. The prize headline was 'France Avenges Waterloo'.

The last match of our marathon British Isles tour was against the British Barbarians at Cardiff Arms Park, a game arranged to finance our visit to both the United States and Canada on our way home. I was privileged to be selected to play in this historic game. The Barbarians game was to become a regular event, and this inaugural game against an international team proved to be fast, open, and played in a wonderful spirit. The Barbarians team that took the field before a crowd of 45 000 included six internationals from England, five from Wales, two from Scotland, one from Ireland, and with the Blackheath winger, Martin Turner, the only uncapped player, virtually a British Lions line-up. The score was 3–3 at half-time, a try to the Ba Bas — the Olympic sprinter C.B. Holmes centre-kicking and Micky Steel-Bodger chasing the loose ball and controlling it with his feet to touch down. Australia's points came from a penalty goal from the touch line by Arthur Tonkin, that bounced off the crossbar.

Some magnificent moves followed in the second half, with Holmes scoring after Welsh centre Bleddyn Williams had cut the Wallaby defence to link up with his forwards. Haydn Tanner, the great Welsh half-back, instigated the third try by the Barbarians and was on the spot to finish it. The Wallabies fought back, with Tonkin outrunning his rivals for a try, but it was a 9–6 victory for the Barbarians, and the crowd surged onto the field to cheer the players. At the after-match dinner in which the Wallabies were toasted, Bill McLean, our tour captain, was honoured with membership of the Barbarians.

The game was such a success that it became scheduled in every touring country's itinerary of the United Kingdom.

We sailed for New York a few days later on board the *Queen Mary*. I was seasick for the entire voyage, but not too sick to enjoy the sight of New York with its huge buildings lit up as we sailed into the harbour at night. We then travelled across the Rockies by train, and at each stop indulged in free-for-all snow fights.

We won our games easily, although most of our opponents were gridiron footballers and the odd expatriate who managed to knock us down whether we had the ball or not. In Los Angeles for the match against the University of California, we were thrilled to meet Joey Brown, the comedian and actor. In San Francisco at 9 p.m. on 21 March 1948 we boarded the four-engine Australian National Airlines Skymaster *Amana* for the long journey home to Australia. We had farewelled team-mate Doug Keller, who returned to Britain for further studies. This plane was to take us to Hawaii, where we stayed overnight, a refuel stop at Canton Island, then an overnight stop in Fiji, where we were entertained by the rugby fraternity. One Fijian who was a sporting enthusiast asked me if we had a 'joker' named Don Bradman in our team!

Arriving in Sydney on 28 March we bade farewell to our team-mates and enjoyed the homecoming with our families. I was saddened to learn that the *Amana*, the plane we flew home in — my first-ever flight — crashed in June 1950 on a scheduled flight from Perth to Melbourne in timbered country on track to Kalgoorlie in Western Australia, killing 29 people. The plane burst into flames on impact and was destroyed.

The 1947–48 Wallabies team was probably the finest side I played in, and the marathon nine-month tour ensured several lasting friendships. At the time of writing, ten of our players have passed away and the remainder meet every year, some in wheelchairs and others with lapses of memory. We have relived countless happy moments over and over. As a young man, that tour taught me many things. It gave me an education I hadn't had, and, above all, it taught me respect and manners.

RUGBY FLASHBACK

Doug Keller, a team-mate from the 1947–48 Tour who went to Britain to further his medical studies and later captained Scotland, played for his Sydney club, Eastwood, against Randwick at Coogee Oval upon his return to Australia. We both found ourselves on the bottom of a fairly fierce ruck when he said that Marcel, his wife, had delivered twin boys that morning. Oblivious of flying boots, we hugged each other in celebration.

---

5 GETTING DOWN TO BUSINESS

My parents' plan for me to learn the dry-cleaning trade had been interrupted by my football career. On my return to Australia in 1948 at the end of my first international tour, I had to think about making a living. At the time, my older sister Alice was a shop assistant, Paulette was a stenographer and George and Margaret were still at school.

My family moved to Blenheim Street in Randwick after the Housing Commission resumed and demolished our home in Redfern. Lots of history and memories were destroyed with that house. It was a sad occasion, as my grandparents had lived there since 1920 and my parents since 1935. The church was rebuilt nearby, but it didn't include a home.

I didn't want to return to Bathurst and the dry-cleaning business and thought it made sense to capitalise on my sporting connections in the Randwick area of Sydney by starting up my own menswear business there. I first gained a little experience in the menswear business by working on Saturday mornings for the Scarfe Brothers, who were family friends, in Auburn. You needed 'key' money in those days (you paid the landlord a sum upfront), and I needed to raise something like £600 by borrowing funds. I didn't know much about business, but I managed to open a shop, which I called Nick Shehadie's Menswear, in Belmore Road, the main street of Randwick. I would buy the stock from various wholesalers.

Soon after I opened the shop, it was broken into. The thieves broke a few windows and stole a good deal of my stock. I just had to put it down to experience — things could only get better.

I knew nothing about accountancy or bookkeeping in those days. I thought that running a business was all just commonsense: if I had money in the bank, and didn't owe any, I figured I was in front. That's how I ran my business at the time. I learned as I went along, and I was fortunate in later life, after I retired from football, to be involved with three commercial boards — one manufacturing, one marketing, and the third, finance — which gave me an overall background to the workings of business.

In 1949, 1952 and 1955 I toured New Zealand with the Australian rugby team. These tours lasted six weeks and we travelled the country from top to bottom. We had great success in 1949, although we didn't play against the number-one New Zealand team who at the time were touring South Africa. But because the New Zealand team's

---

RUGBY FLASHBACK

In 1949, playing the West Coast at Greymouth in New Zealand, the referee, Bob Pratt, penalised our big forward, Roger Cornforth, for being punched in the mouth, then ordered Wallaby team-mate, Bev Wilson, off the field. Don Furness, the master of intrigue, said to the referee, 'Don't send him off. Give him a spell on the sideline.' And the referee did!

Maori players were forbidden to tour there, some say we ended up playing against a better team than the one that toured South Africa. We defeated New Zealand 2–0 to win the Bledisloe Cup.

Touring New Zealand is a wonderful experience — it completes one's education in rugby. We were managed by two former international players, Ron Walden, who was chief of the Criminal Investigation Bureau (CIB) in Sydney at the time, and Bill Cerruti, one of rugby's greatest characters and players.

After that tour we all settled back into our everyday way of life, going to work each day and down to the beach at weekends. Colin Windon, who was a regular visitor to the races and later a prominent horse-owner, rang me late one Saturday afternoon to tell me that he had won a handsome sum at the races that afternoon, and asked me to join him at one of the fashionable nightclubs (now known as bars) in Double Bay. Having no funds myself, I agreed. Col picked me up in his big, but not-too-new, orange twin-door Packard with a dinky seat at the back. On arriving at the club at about 8.30 p.m.,

RUGBY FLASHBACK

In 1949, with the New Zealand Maoris touring team in Australia, the Australian Rugby Union decided to place microphones along the touchlines. Sydney Cricket Ground officials came from everywhere to remove the microphones after Kingi Mathews, the Maori hooker, called out from the scrum, 'Put the f...ing ball in!' His voice had carried all over the ground.

we went upstairs to a private room, which was packed with people having a good time. The bar was very busy and the piano belted out all the popular tunes of the day.

At about 11 p.m. there was a huge bang when the bar doors were suddenly thrown open by two huge, plainclothes policemen. 'Nobody move!' they shouted. Apparently it was illegal to sell liquor on the premises. Col and I got the shock of our lives when we saw that the cops were in fact Ron Waldren, who had managed our New Zealand tour some weeks earlier, and his partner, Frank ('Bumper') Farrell, a former great Rugby League player. When they spotted us among the nervous patrons, Ron called again, 'Nobody move!' Then he came over to us and whispered, 'You two, buzz off.' And we did. Ron wasn't only a good cop, he was a good bloke. We never went back to that club.

Early in 1951, we lost our father. He was fifty-six. My mother's doctor, Alex Moir, called in every morning to have coffee with her. My father had been somewhere to assist a new immigrant and,

RUGBY FLASHBACK

In 1951 when the All Blacks were on their Australian tour, the Australian Rugby Union had arranged for them to play an Invitation Fifteen on the Melbourne Cricket Ground. Players were invited from every state; only Alan Cameron and myself were then current Test players. Each time we kicked off, the All Blacks seemed to score, racking up more than fifty points. After the match, Kevin Skinner, the very rugged All Black prop, joined me in a drink, but then said we were becoming too friendly. He said it would 'be on' in the next Test. We shook hands on it. The Test was a week later in Brisbane and I didn't have to wait long before he delivered a great whack, the legacy being a thick left ear that I still carry around. But, yes, we are still good friends.

when he returned home, he opened the door and fell inside, suffering a massive heart attack. Dr Moir, who was there at the time, pronounced him dead. His death greatly affected our family, not least because he had been in debt and owed money on our house. But this was to bring our family even closer together. We made the decision to work together to pay off the debt.

After running the menswear shop successfully for three years, I knew I would have no trouble selling the business. In 1951 I sold it and purchased with my brother a dry-cleaning business in the western Sydney suburb of Lidcombe. I could see the chance of making higher returns in the new business, and I liked the idea of the family working together. George had become quite experienced in the dry-cleaning business, having trained in the Sydney area prior to coming in with me.

George and Alice and I would leave Randwick at five o'clock every morning. George did the pressing with me and another staff member, Trevor King, who later became an Australian boxing champion, did the cleaning. Alice ran the counter. We had several depots from which I used to go around collecting and delivering clothes. We worked hard and watched our costs. George and I were partners — and we still are.

We grew that business and eventually sold it in 1954. We were able to pay off all our family's financial commitments, which had been the family priority before going into business together. It was a great feeling not to owe anyone any money. For my mother, in particular, who had been very concerned about the family's debts, it was a tremendous relief.

6 SOUTH AFRICAN TOUR, 1953

Australia hadn't visited South Africa since 1933 — tours didn't take place as frequently as they do now, plus the Second World War had been fought in the intervening years — so it was with some excitement that I prepared for our 1953 tour of the Republic in my role as vice-captain to the skipper, John Solomon. I felt some concern, though, because of my dark complexion and Lebanese background. Would I be admitted into the country or be embarrassed there by their apartheid system? I requested that the Australian Rugby Union check out this situation before leaving, and they assured me that everything would be okay.

George and Alice insisted that I go on the tour, telling me that they could carry on and manage the business while I was away. I felt a little guilty about being away for five months. It was very generous of them.

After the team was selected we still had a few weeks to go until we were to leave for the tour. Wally Meagher, the coach at Randwick, ran several coaching sessions for the Sydney team members at the request of Johnny Wallace, our assistant manager and coach. Wally had toured with the 1927 Waratahs under Johnny's captaincy. Wally told us that we would hate our tour manager, Wylie ('Breck') Breckenridge for the first few months, but that then we would walk up walls for him. He was such an abrupt and up-front man at times but he had a heart of gold. We did learn to love him, as Wally had predicted — he knew his stuff and was such a genuine guy. At all the dances in South Africa, he would get on the microphone and demand that the ladies dance with 'all my boys'. Then he'd say, 'You will learn to love my boys!' We certainly loved him.

On our arrival in Johannesburg, Australia's world-champion boxer, Jimmy Carruthers, and his manager, Bill McConnell, were among the thousands who greeted us at the airport. Jimmy had just won the world championship, defeating Willie Towell of South Africa. The Lebanese community was there in force and I discovered later that some of them had asked Breck whether I was married. I am sure they had ideas to match me up during the tour.

The hospitality we were shown in South Africa was outstanding — we were welcomed everywhere. We made an early visit to the

RUGBY FLASHBACK

My favourite rugby story involved Bill Cerutti, probably the most popular footballer ever to pull on an Australian jersey. He toured South Africa in 1933 and related later that the matches preceding the first Test were tough, rough and quite dirty. So, it was decided to bring both teams together at a dinner and read them the Riot Act. It went something like this. The president of the South African Rugby Union said that any Springbok who didn't play the game in the right spirit wouldn't play again for his country. Then the Australian manager, Dr Mathews, said that any Australian player who misbehaved on the field and not in the true rugby spirit would be sent home. The two famous South African brothers, Boy and Fanny Louw, were in the front row, and the pair whispered to Bill Cerutti, 'It'll be on tomorrow.' Bill replied, 'Why wait for tomorrow?' and an all-in brawl broke out, with Aub Hodgson supporting 'Wild Bill'.

Kruger National Park, which, by day, was an adventure; at night, sleeping was a little scary with the cries of wild animals resounding around our compound. The countryside reminded us very much of Australia with all the gum trees, species that had been introduced there years before.

John Solomon, the tour captain, fell ill prior to the start of the tour, so, as the vice-captain of the touring team, I took over the responsibilities of captaining the side until John returned to the side seven matches later. We opened our tour in Durban, where we had assembled two weeks prior to the first match. It was here that our team put on lifesaving exhibitions on the beach several times for the local surf clubs. Fourteen of us were members of surf clubs at home and, equipped with Australian costumes supplied by lifesaving authorities before we left, we gave demonstrations of march-pasts and surf rescues Australian-style.

South African rugby was very physical — it was nothing like we had ever experienced before, with more body contact and less rucking. Our opponents were very big men, and their style of play relied heavily on the forwards to control the match. The scrummaging was fierce and, at times, brutal. I am sure their front-rowers were the first players selected, with the rest of the team selected around them. Men such as Jaap Becker, Chris Koch, Bubbles Koch, Salty du Rand and Ernest Dinkleman were all giants. Several of us later had to have minor surgery done on our rectums, the result of relentless hard pushing.

The game at Port Elizabeth saw me captain Australia for the first time in a Test match, with John Solomon sidelined. We lost, but it was a close, torrid match. The four points awarded at the time for field goals did not assist us.

Newlands, Capetown, 5 September 1953, and the rugby world was about to be turned on its head. We were witnessing the conquest of the mighty South African Springboks, invincible for eighteen long years, victors in eleven successive Test matches against all-comers, and, finally, overthrown in an incredible contest by us, known as the Australian Wallaby 'battlers'.

I recall the action as vividly as though it were yesterday. I was

On the bowling green in the Orange Free State, South Africa, in 1953. From left: Jack Blomley; one of our South African hosts; Brian Johnson; Dave Brockhoff; John Solomon; and me.

one of fourteen Australian players standing transfixed around our own 25-yard line, yelling and screaming, 'Go, go, go!' as our red-headed winger, Garth Jones, raced down the left wing touch line. The Springbok captain, Hennie Muller, the speediest cover defending forward in the world at the time, was in hot pursuit — just a stride separated the pair. Jones pulled away, made it to the South African goal line and flung himself onto the turf, exhausted but triumphant, and the Wallabies snatched the lead that would give them the Test match 18–14.

John Solomon's 1953 tourists had arrived in the Republic on a hazardous mission, with Springbok rugby at its peak following an all-conquering tour of the British Isles by Basil Kenyon's team two years earlier, in 1951. The 'Boks had demolished the four Home counties and the French, and when the South African selectors announced their line-up to play the Wallabies, all fifteen players came out of that 1951 touring team.

During the tour we visited Rhodesia, now known as Zimbabwe, and we witnessed the awesome spectacle of the Victoria Falls and other tourist attractions. In Kitwe, in northern Rhodesia, together with Spanner Brown, I was billeted with the Thomas family (there was never a hotel big enough to fit all the team and entourage), a most hospitable and friendly family who lived in a huge house with many servants. They made me several offers to return and work in the variety of companies they owned. This was very tempting at the time. I was young and ambitious, but I owed it to my brother and sister to return to Sydney.

Our Wallabies made stuttering progress across the veldt, sharing victories with unnerving defeats at the hands and boots of powerful provincial and university combinations. It seemed the Wallabies needed to start from scratch in their scrummaging and lineout work. Dr Danie Craven, guru of South African rugby, followed our tour progress closely and wrote in his book, *Springbok Story*: 'Here you have the Wallabies. They could play brilliantly and they could play badly. Their matches produced bright, very bright, moments, and also dull, very dull, moments. When you expected something from them, it never came, and when you were not expecting it, you would be surprised. Most unpredictable they were.'

Early predictions and fears were realised when we lost the first Test at Ellis Park with a 25–3 score line — we were simply scrummed into the ground. And there was also Johannesburg's high altitude — we couldn't breathe! The Springbok pack was massive in size and ferociously strong. In the front row, our props Bob Davidson and Jack Carroll were in the firing line where their opposite numbers, Chris Koch and Jaap Bekker, hammered them. Bekker was intimidatingly powerful, reportedly training with a rock and chain around his neck, and succeeding in snapping a goalpost and breaking the backs of a couple of rivals. In the later Tests I had to move into the front row. Recognising the prospect of being ground into the turf, I developed a technique of pushing my head straight into his neck so that he couldn't move me. It worked, even if I did finish the series with a split backside.

The first Test team was chosen during our tour break in the Kruger National Park, and we probably erred in selecting our heaviest available line-up in a bid to match the Springbok heavyweights. We were finding it difficult to breathe easily in the high-altitude environment of Johannesburg, so we adopted new tactics for the second Test. With mobile flanker Brian Johnson, half-back Cyril Burke, five-eighth Spanner Brown, prop Col Forbes and full-back Ray Colbert chosen, Tony Miller moved into the second row from the lock position. This was a team picked for pace — lighter, but quicker, designed to move their big forwards around and exploiting our quick hands.

Suddenly, there was a new enthusiasm in our ranks, a spark in the team, and we felt we were in with a chance. Nobody else did, of course, but there was another factor in our favour: the South African public was tiring of the Springboks' concentration on heavy

Murray Tate (left) and I exchange jerseys after the Wallabies' game against the South African Universities in Cape Town in 1953. We were well beaten by the students in that game and, indeed, victories were hard to come by with Springbok football at its peak, but our famous Second Test victory at Newlands a week later was about to brighten our tour.

scrummaging and line-kicking. Breck, our manager, would upset the South African diehards by saying that he had daughters who could kick a football out all day. The Wallabies were winning fans with our efforts to play bright football and to carry the ball, not just kick it.

Scoring three fine tries, the Springboks made a dazzling start to the second Test, but then their play lost momentum — even though they held an 11–3 lead at half-time. Yet another try by us made it 14–8, but the turning point of the match arrived with the Wallabies scoring twice from inside their own half. For the next twenty minutes we were to endure a Springbok attack like we had never experienced before, and we held fast. How we did it, I don't know. We were weary and desperate, but we wouldn't give in. It was all blood and guts. On one occasion, Chris Koch, the huge Springbok front-rower, dived over our line, but somehow I managed to dive under him, stop the ball being grounded, and save the try. We were determined to stop them from scoring, and finally a quick heel came our way.

With a minute to go, we won the loose ball from a ruck with Spanner Brown gathering just 10 yards from our line. The Australian captain, John Solomon, had earlier left the field with an injury. (The no-replacement rule applied.) He returned, taking up a position as an extra centre in a back line and driving us like never before — Ed Stapleton had moved into the centre and Brian Johnson to the wing. Two South African defenders made the mistake of targeting Stapleton, leaving space for Garth Jones on the left wing. The Welsh writer J.B.G. Thomas described what followed:

When Jones received the ball, he was quite sixty yards from the Springbok line, but Muller was coming across to get him. After the match, Muller said he felt it was best to keep inside Jones and pace it out with him in the hope that he would tackle him before he reached the line. However, although Muller gained at first, Jones suddenly opened the gap between them. On, on he went, with the crowd on its feet and yelling itself hoarse. This was the try of the series, as eventually the Queensland flyer crossed the line, swung in beautifully to put the ball down behind the South African goalposts. Colbert came up to convert the try and the final whistle went for full-time. Australia had pulled off a fabulous victory. The world champions had been beaten on their own turf and although there was criticism of the South African methods, there was no doubting the right of Australia to win the match. Their open play blazed a trail across South Africa, where we were called 'The Waltzing Wallabies'.

Danie Craven seemed just a little miffed about John Solomon's role in the victory. Solomon was too clever for the Springboks. Craven wrote:

> He [Solomon] got hurt, or so he pretended. In any case he left the field and soon came back. Keeping up the act he retained the fast Brian Johnson on the wing and Stapleton at centre, he himself hobbling round as third or roving centre. When he got the ball it was obvious that if he had got hurt it had not impaired his speed in the slightest. With this extra back, the Wallabies scored their last two tries.

Solomon subsequently stoutly denied Craven's claim.

Craven's account of this memorable Test makes interesting reading.

> I tried to analyse the match for the causes which inhibited the Springboks from reproducing their overseas form. It was

obvious that they were not as fit as they used to be; that they did not have the same combination and feeling for one another's play; that they all had workaday jobs and could not devote the same time to the game without any worries; that they were two years older, and so on.

In the second place, the white jerseys they had to wear was something foreign to a team which had played thirty-one times before in the green, which is the ambition of every South African to wear. There was just no sentiment attached to a white jersey with a ghastly badge on the left breast ... the white jersey had other drawbacks — the players were used to green and when they looked for somebody in support and there was a fellow in green they might pass out to him or they might well hesitate before looking for someone else. Passes were given to the Wallabies on at least three occasions when the Springboks were dangerous. It is not for me to suggest the Wallabies alter their colours. All I know is that both in 1933 and 1937 they played in light blue, the colours of the Waratahs. It is certain that we played in green before them, but Ireland had their light green before us. They refused to play in white against us in 1906 and 1912, but they did so, however, in 1931 and 1951.

Craven must have forgotten that Australia played in white in 1956 when the Springboks toured Australia.

Finally, he wrote: '... the new demand by the public for open rugby created uncertainty among our players ...'

Danie Craven, together with so many other diehard South African supporters, took the defeat hard, but it was pure champagne for us. We lost the series, but that defeat by the Wallabies of the 'Boks and the sight of Garth Jones in his breathtaking match-winning scamper down the wing will live on.

It was a truly famous victory.

7 MARRIAGE

Marie and I did not meet again until 1953, following my return from the Wallabies' tour of South Africa. Marie was by then a medical student, and a resident at Women's College at the University of Sydney. The college had a visionary policy of encouraging international women scholars to join the college community during their postgraduate studies. One of that talented group was Mercedes Concepcion, known as Ditas, a Colombo Plan graduate from the Philippines, who was studying advanced prostatistics at the university.

Accompanied by Ditas, Marie had made a visit one weekend afternoon to her Aunt Rose in Coogee. Quite out of the blue, while driving the girls back to college, Rose decided to call in to see my mother at our home in Randwick.

Rose and my mother chatted away, and I was engaged in conversation with Marie and Ditas. Being sociable, Marie asked me about South Africa. How had I enjoyed the experience, the unique aspects of the culture, the political problems and apartheid? Since she seemed to indicate great interest in my views, I mentioned that in a few weeks' time the team would be having a film night to show family and friends some footage of the tour. It was to be held at the home of Max Elliot, a Sydney University medical student and member of the team. Given her interest, I invited Marie to come along, and she accepted.

I was not thinking of Marie as a potential girlfriend at the time; my mind was on rugby and other responsibilities, such as running my dry-cleaning business. Marie, I am sure, was thinking of her medical studies. Later I learned that she had agreed to go out with me because of the possibility of introducing me to one of her friends whose romance had recently broken up. Apparently she and Ditas considered that I would be the perfect replacement and an excellent match.

On the day that I was to call for her, I rang my friend and teammate Keith Cross, and told him, 'Don't bring a girl tonight — I've invited a girl from Women's College and I want you to help me entertain her.' Keith was one of my closest friends; we had toured together and went on occasional double dates. I did not know Marie very well and worried that she might not be interested in the rugby scene, so I wanted to make sure that she would be looked after and not become bored. Plus, I could relax and have a drink or two with the boys if Keith was around to help look after her.

We collected Marie in Keith's Morris A30 — a small car — and drove to Max's parents' home in the southern Sydney suburb of Carlton. When Max opened the door, he could not conceal his surprise at seeing Marie, saying, 'What are you doing with *him*? You're going out with so and so!' This was news to me.

Marie had previously met three of the players, who were medical students, including the captain John Solomon. Thus they were surprised to see her arrive with me, as they knew the fellow student she had been seeing. They were not aware that I knew her.

It was a lovely, relaxing evening. Afterwards Keith and I took Marie home and I did not think much more of it. Some weeks later, I rang her, because a close friend, another team-mate from the 1947 Wallabies, Arch Winning, had become engaged to a Queensland girl. Her parents were coming to Sydney for the engagement celebration and I was asked to bring a girl to join them for dinner. I was not seeing anyone at the time and asked Marie to join us. The dinner was held at Chequers restaurant and nightclub in the city. However, I told her that she would have to come to the rugby match beforehand since I did not have a car, and I was relying on Arch for transport later on. She hesitated, saying something about having too much ironing to do! To her surprise, I promptly offered to do the ironing for her if she would come. She accepted.

We were playing Manly at Manly Oval. I had never taken a girl to a football match before and Marie really knew nothing about rugby. I happened to score a try and the people around her shouted,

'Nick scored a try!', but even though she was watching, she had not noticed it!

We won the game, and because I had scored the try, people were coming up to congratulate Marie, which made her feel embarrassed. After the match, we went on to dinner. Marie had not met Arch before, and I had made it clear that the whole evening was about doing the right thing by him, in the presence of the future parents-in-law.

Up till this period in my life I had not gone out with many girls; I had been too busy and preoccupied with the challenges ahead. People used to think it odd that Keith Cross and I spent so much time together! After a pleasant evening, I took Marie back to Women's College in a taxi, and then went on home to Randwick.

We saw each other on and off over the next few months, but it was still a somewhat formal but warm friendship. Indeed, I took her out for three months before I kissed her goodnight!

By late 1954, Marie was completing a student paediatrics term at the Royal Alexandria Hospital for Children at Camperdown. As I called to collect her on one particular day, I could see that she was clearly distressed, and asked her the reason. Through tears, she spoke of a two-year-old child, whom she described as 'exquisite', who was suffering from a potentially fatal illness for which surgery was essential. Overwhelmed by this news, the child's family had virtually abandoned her — as a result there were no visitors, no toys, no enquiries about her wellbeing or progress and no permission for surgery, just caring staff who felt absolutely powerless. I could not help but share Marie's distress and sadness.

The next day, without saying anything to Marie, I headed for the toy section of a department store, selected some beautiful toys and arranged for them to be delivered to the hospital. It was several days later, when asking around, that Marie learned who was responsible, commenting that my reaction had reminded her of her father.

I believe that that experience brought us closer. I had no ulterior motive, no wish to impress, but my gift of toys to her little patient, a sad and lovely child, seemed to break any barriers of mistrust that may have existed between us.

George and I had, by now, sold the Lidcombe dry-cleaning business, and I was employed by Wormald Industries as a sales representative for fire doors and security systems. Marie and I continued to see one another regularly over the next two years and steadily became closer. The old family Dodge was our regular transport. The springs had collapsed in the passenger seat, so few people realised that I was courting her, since the front seat passenger could not be seen!

Our relationship was a surprise to many who regarded our interests as quite different. Marie was great to be with. She was well read, more concerned about world issues than me, and a great lover of classical music and opera. She opened my eyes to other areas of life with which I soon became fascinated. We learned much together.

By 1956 our relationship had become more serious and I knew that I wanted to marry her. She had completed her medical studies and was enjoying her appointment as junior resident medical officer at St Vincent's Hospital. We decided that I should ask her parents for permission to marry when next they were visiting Sydney from Narrandera. I booked a table at Kinneil, one of Sydney's most elegant restaurants, located in a beautiful historic home in Potts Point. I had been there with friends several times and although my financial situation could not be described as brilliant at the time, I could afford dinner at a fine restaurant every now and then. As we walked up to the restaurant, Marie's father Michel asked me, 'Do you come here often?'

'No, not at all,' I replied. And as we walked in, the head waiter said, 'Good evening, Mr Shehadie, the usual table?' An awkward moment!

Marie and I had arranged that when the time came for coffee following the meal, she would invite her mother, Victoria, to accompany her to the powder room, so that I could speak discreetly with her father, and put my question. I was certainly on edge, and didn't know what to expect. Marie was a medical doctor; I was a footballer and sales representative.

When the time for coffee arrived, Victoria declined the cue to visit the powder room. As I just sat there Marie kicked me under the table. With everyone present, my confidence to ask simply deserted me.

When dinner was finished I paid the bill. After bidding goodnight to the head waiter, we drove with Marie's parents to the waterfront at Elizabeth Bay in my old Holden. Marie kept nudging me, and I kept whispering protests that it was not the right time.

We then drove to Grandma Melick's house, where Marie's parents were staying. As we knocked at the door, Aunt Marie, one of the family's favourite aunts and a great influence on the younger Marie,

A momentous day in my life. On 23 February 1957, a three-year courtship with Marie Bashir culminates in our marriage at St Philips Church, Sydney. Here, Marie signs the register. In the background are my mother (left) and Marie's sister Helen.

called out 'Congratulations, congratulations!' She had known of our plans ... but not of our failure to carry through. The women rushed out to the kitchen, while I sat, greatly embarrassed, with Marie's father in the lounge room. I was then able to summon up the courage to say to him, 'Marie and I would like to get married.'

Michel then proceeded to lecture me for the next forty-five minutes about how special his daughter was, and how footballers 'get fat and go to seed after a while'. Patiently, I waited for his answer. Finally, I said, 'You haven't replied "yes" or "no", Sir.'

He said, 'Oh, that doesn't matter.' He needed to make the speech. He was a prominent member of Rotary and really enjoyed making speeches. He had had this one ready for some time — our marriage intentions had in fact become common knowledge among our families. We were overjoyed.

We were married at the historic St Philips Church, Sydney, on 23 February 1957, and the reception for 200 guests was held at Glen Ascham, a grand private hotel in Darling Point which has since disappeared in the redevelopment of Sydney. It was a great party. My brother, George, acted as best man, and Marie's sister Helen and five of her cousins were the bridesmaids. The marriage ceremony was conducted by the Reverend Dr Felix Arnott, the Warden of St Paul's College at Sydney University, who later became the Archbishop of Brisbane.

Dr Denby Bowdler, a close friend of ours, proposed the toast to the bride and groom, and set the mood for a memorable evening. Tragically, Denby was killed with some family members years later, in a midair collision over Zagreb.

I felt exceedingly happy. My parents-in-law were abundantly warm and generous. It was interesting also to observe the strong and affectionate relationship that developed between my mother and my wife.

It was possibly a coincidence that Marie and I have the same cultural background. Indeed, each of us has always had an intensely strong sense of Australian identity.

We spent our honeymoon driving through Tasmania. Because of the forthcoming selection for the tour of Great Britain, France and North America, I maintained my daily training regimen. Marie was always supportive.

After the wedding we lived for a short period in Kirribilli, at the northern end of the Sydney Harbour Bridge, where I continued my training routine obsessively. I was aware that no other player had made two tours to the British Isles as a Wallaby ten years apart. If included in the touring team, I was also elated at the thought that Marie may join me in London.

8 SECOND WALLABIES INTERNATIONAL TOUR, 1957–58

The 1957 rugby season wasn't an easy time for me. At club level, I had learned that Cyril Towers, then a Randwick Club selector, wanted me out of the first-grade team, particularly as captain. Dick Tooth, a personal friend of mine, had joined Randwick from Sydney University and Cyril wanted him as first-grade captain, hoping that he would go on and captain the touring team to the United Kingdom later that year. Cyril just didn't expect me to be selected for two tours ten years apart. Randwick's policy was for the players to elect the captain, and if I were graded in reserve grade I wouldn't be a threat.

With the prospect of being relegated to the reserves, I told our president, Wally Meagher, that I would be leaving the club and turning out across the harbour with Northern Suburbs Club. Wally said to me that Randwick was my club and he would insist that I stay. He went on to say that if I was relegated to the reserves, he would call me prior to the teams being announced. He did, and confirmed that I was in the seconds, but urged me not to leave the club because I was about to be chosen in the South Harbour representative team fixture a week later. (In those days, South Harbour versus North Harbour was the fixture at which the city team was selected.) How he knew this I didn't know. Having the utmost respect for Wally's judgment, I took his advice and stayed, and played in the seconds against Eastern Suburbs. I had an awful match, but Wally knew something and I was duly selected for South Harbour. I was then restored to the Randwick first fifteen and went on to play all the representative games.

Dick Tooth, together with Randwick stalwart and very mobile back-rower Keith Cross, were shock omissions from the 1957–58 Wallaby touring team (for which we would pay dearly on the British tour).

Cyril Towers and I were never close; I don't know why. I'm sure he felt that forwards were a different breed. Interestingly, Cyril never coached a Randwick first-grade team.

The 1957–58 tour (I did, in fact, become the first player to tour ten years apart) was a huge disappointment for me, having experienced the thrill and success of playing with the 1947–48 Wallabies. This time we just weren't winning our share of matches

RUGBY FLASHBACK

On the eve of my departure for my second Wallaby tour of the British Isles, I was described in a newspaper as 'Sentimental Nick'. I confess that I was sentimental in requesting jersey No. 24 for the tour, the same number that I wore throughout the 1947–48 tour a decade earlier. The Australian Rugby Union agreed, although No. 24 placed me among the back-row forwards on the team's official list, whereas I had been chosen this time as a front-row prop. There was a delay in taking the official photograph of the touring team before we left, as I had to go to court to face a parking charge.

Our baggage for the tour included the issue of two blazers, a pair of grey slacks, four green ties with a hand-painted Wallaby on each, a heavy pullover and a track suit. In addition, each player received one pair of boots — with another pair to be issued in England — sandshoes for training on the ship, a heavy woollen scarf, plus tablets to counteract seasickness, Vitamin C tablets to counteract colds in Britain and a packet of tranquilliser tablets — 'to be used at the player's own discretion'.

and there wasn't the same feeling of commitment. I felt that the managers, Terry McClenaughan and Dave Cowper, had a different level of commitment to that of Arnold Tancred, who put winning matches before anything else. I don't think we were fit, and our training was devoid of variety, which made it very tedious. I remember that at Gosforth, near Newcastle in the north of

England, the coach, Dave Cowper, was running the team and he only had two moves: 'Ruck it here ... ruck it there.' Jim Brown, our number-one hooker, looking openly disgusted, said to him, 'Ruck it your bloody self' and walked off the field. Later, two of our most seasoned players, Alan Cameron and Tony Miller, confessed that they, too, were growing increasingly disappointed with the way the tour was going.

The Test against Ireland at Lansdowne Road, Dublin, should have been a memorable one for me, as it turned out to be my last Test appearance. Well, it *was* memorable, but not exactly for the right reasons, because I got mixed up in an awful incident — one I have never been proud of. Packing on the loose head side of the scrum, Noel Murphy, the Irish breakaway, was constantly putting his hand over my eyes so that I couldn't see the ball being put into the scrum. Jim Brown, my hooker, said, 'Hang one on him.' As we broke up after one scrum, I warned Murphy that if he did it again I would deal with him. When he ignored my warning and did it again, I landed a punch that Mohammed Ali would have been proud of. It laid him out cold on the turf. Fellow Wallaby John Thornett, who was packing on that side of the scrum, was probably the only person who saw it happen; the referee, who was on the blind side of the scrum, certainly didn't see it, though he penalised us 'on suspicion'. Murphy came to and kept his hands away from my eyes during the rest of the match. However, from the penalty an 'up and under' was taken by Ireland, aimed at me. With the forwards charging down, I stood my ground, waiting for the mighty hit, but it didn't come, as one of my team-mates interfered (illegally), with the front-row forward charging down on me and blocking the charge. I was safe, but we were penalised.

After the match Dave Cowper said that it had been a vicious thing for me to do, but he was on the other side of the ground and was in no position to see the incident. He told me that I wouldn't be playing in any future Test matches — and he didn't select me. The Lansdowne crowd of some 40 000 booed the team, and I was singled out, with one Irish newspaper commenting that the two most hated men ever to come to Ireland were Oliver Cromwell and Nick Shehadie. Noel Murphy was later to become president of the Irish Rugby Union. Today he and I are good friends, while Tony O'Reilly, now 'Sir Anthony', who played in that international and whom I see from time to time, never allows me to forget the incident. It wasn't a pleasant time, but the team stuck by me.

At the end of the tour, the now established Barbarians match took place, and because I had made two tours to the United Kingdom and had played in the original game a decade earlier, I was invited to play, this time for the Ba Bas against my own touring team at Cardiff Arms Park. Our managers were very generous in allowing this — I was surprised that they agreed after my previous experience in Ireland. No other player had ever been honoured in this way until, a few years later, Ian Clarke of New Zealand played against his own touring All Blacks during their British tour.

The Barbarians assembled on the Friday before the match in Penarth, a seaside suburb of Cardiff just outside the city centre. (Marie was to travel to London, but wives and girlfriends were not offically allowed to join the touring team.) My allocated room-mate was Ron Jacobs, the then English prop forward, who later became president of England Rugby. Many great British and Irish players were in that team, notably Cliff Morgan, Andy Mulligan, Michael Phillips, Tony O'Reilly, Ron Dawson, David Marques, Adam Robson and Arthur Smith. I shall always remember the team talk prior to our leaving for the ground. The president, Brigadier Glyn Hughes, affectionately known as 'Hughie', addressed the team with whisky in hand by saying, 'Gentlemen, today we play Australia and we want you to play in the true Ba Ba spirit and bring the best out of the Australians. Shehadie, you may now purchase a tie; and Morgan, you will captain the team.' Well, we beat the Wallabies and at the end of the game we all sang 'Auld Lang Syne', and I was carried shoulder-high off the field. It was a fast and open game and I was getting that little extra treatment from my touring team-mates — the odd jab in the ribs, but all in jest, of course!

Marie and I had married just prior to the tour, and (thanks largely to her generous parents) she was present to see me being honoured in this way, something I will cherish all my life. She had been invited to the match as the guest of Hughie's wife, Thelma.

Recently, Tony O'Reilly remembered my contribution to the match with these words:

> On the wall in my office ... is a photograph of the Barbarians vs. Australia game of January 1958. Some of the truly greats of yesteryear stare out at one ... But at the end of the seated row sits the most unusual Barbarian of all, Nicholas Shehadie. I say 'unusual' not just because he was such a fine player, but because

Acknowledging the crowd's ovation at Cardiff Arms Park — what a way to wind up my rugby career. That evening, both teams attended a dinner and I sat as a Barbarian alongside an Australian colleague. It was a great honour.

The climax of my thirty-Test rugby career arrived with my appearance for the British Barbarians against my own touring team, the 1957–58 Wallabies, at the Cardiff Arms Park, Wales. It was the first time a tour player had been invited to join the Barbarians against his fellow tourists. Many famous players took the field, and the Ba Bas won 11–6 in a thriller. Players from both sides in this encounter came together for this photograph.

he was a member of that Wallabies touring team and yet was given the singular honour of playing for the Barbarians against Australia in the final match of the tour.

It seems to me symbolic of both Shehadie and of the game of rugby. The rules for the Barbarians are simple; they are two in number: you have to be a footballer and a gentleman. Shehadie is both. And the Barbarians in their wisdom conferred on him the honour of being the first ever tourist to these shores selected to play in the final match of each tour *for* the Barbarians rather than *against* them.

For Nick, it was the crowning moment of a great affair that had started twelve years earlier when he was one of the youngest players selected for the first Australian team to tour these shores in the post-war years in 1947–48. I saw them play at Lansdowne Road as an eleven-year-old ... They beat Ireland 16–3 on that day ...

For a boy from a Lebanese family that went to Australia seeking new horizons, he is the epitome to me of all that is good, fine, noble and humorous about Australia and its rugby football. They don't come better.

On this second tour of the United Kingdom, our pocket money had climbed to ten shillings a day — up from five shillings a decade before! We always travelled first-class, so we weren't lacking in comforts, but no one in those days played for money; there just wasn't any to be had from the game. We played for the honour and enjoyment of the competition, and the camaraderie. The hospitality and team friendships were worth more than hard cash could have compensated for. Rugby today is a full-time professional job, and I feel sure that a lot of the fun has gone out of the game. I feel privileged to have played with and against wonderful people in an era when the true spirit of competition was still intact. Wally Meagher and Len Palfreyman from the Randwick club were great teachers and role models.

After touring the United States and Canada we returned home, where I decided to retire from the game. I was suffering from various injuries, including a dislocated shoulder. I had played thirty Test matches for Australia, a record at the time, and had the privilege of making six overseas Wallaby tours. Being invited to play with the British Barbarians against my own Australian touring team capped off my career. I think most sportspeople know when it's time to retire. I felt that I was slowing up, and the touring was becoming a little tedious.

Rugby played a big part in my life in many ways. It taught me many things. Not least, it opened my eyes to a broad cross-section of people whom otherwise I would not have had the opportunity to meet. As a newly married man, it was now time to go on to other things and take on new responsibilities.

Sir Wilson Whineray, friend and former New Zealand captain, summed up my rugby career with the following generous words:

My first meeting with Nick Shehadie was relatively violent. I was playing in my first Test match versus Australia in 1957. Among the many fine Wallaby forwards playing that day was

Nick, who had the well-earned reputation of being one of the finest tight forwards in the rugby world.

He had been playing for Australia for about ten years and was respected for his tough and unbending approach, his skill and ability to play the full eighty minutes — yet always within the laws and spirit of the game, and always with style.

At kick-off, the ball floated towards me. I knew that it, a bunch of Wallaby forwards and I would meet up at the same time. A jarring tackle, a shake-up in the ensuing ruck, was my welcome to Test match rugby. My enduring memory was looking up, from the ground, into Nick's piercing eyes, which proclaimed that there was more of this to come. We spoke at length after the game, a conversation both pleasant and helpful.

Nick retired from rugby the following year and began a life outside of rugby that was multi-faceted and remarkably successful ...

It was my privilege to play against Nick and to enjoy his company in the years that followed. He was a jewel in the crown of rugby and one who made a significant contribution to Sydney and Australia in many ways over many years.

My rib is still a little painful at times, but at least I can say, 'Nick Shehadie did that — but he did it with kindness.'

These days I look foward to our reunions — where the stories are still the same, but far more exaggerated.

9 SETTLING DOWN

Marie and I were living in a flat in Roslyn Gardens, Elizabeth Bay, when our first child, Michael, was born on 2 February 1959. I rang my mother-in-law, Victoria, who was visiting from Narrandera and seeing her sister Millie, who lived just a few doors from my mother in Blenheim Street, Randwick, to tell her the news. She was so excited that she left me hanging on the phone while she ran up the street to tell my mother.

Michael was a robust baby, if nowhere near his dad's hefty birth weight. He was named after my late father, and my mother utterly spoiled him.

I was back in my job at Wormald Industries selling fire doors and security systems, but I needed to borrow some money, because we needed a bigger house — we knew we wanted to have more children. After Michael's birth I borrowed £125 from my brother, George, for the deposit on a house in Pendle Hill, which in those days was in the far western suburbs of Sydney. Our house, like its neighbours, was built of fibro, and had a huge back yard and an outside toilet — the council would come and empty the loo once a week.

During this time, I was head-hunted from Wormald to join an asphalt company as sales manager. Joining that company was certainly not one of my better decisions. At Wormald I had become the personnel manager, a position which I enjoyed. The new job meant that I was responsible for asphalt and vinyl tile orders from builders and architects. Soon after I started I grew unhappy with the way the company was run. I'd had experience selling to architects during my Wormald days, but this job, and the company itself, just wasn't what I was expecting. Even though the new position involved a promotion and I was offered many incentives, I only stayed there for ten months.

Marie became pregnant with Susan during this time. Soon after we moved to Pendle Hill, the local pharmacist built her a surgery next to his business and she began practice as a general practitioner. She was on her own, and was very busy and worked extremely long hours. Two years later, Alexandra was born.

Marie delivered lots of children during this period and regularly forgot to charge her patients. Instead, we were kept in chickens —

people would often leave them at our door as a gesture of thanks. Many people in the area — Maltese, in particular — had chicken farms.

I decided to leave the asphalt company and venture once more into business on my own. In 1961 I registered Nicholas Shehadie Pty Ltd, a company that supplied and fixed vinyl tiles. It was a risk I wanted to take. I wanted to feel in control of my life. Not owning a car, and occupying tiny, cheap premises (£2 per week in rent), a shopfront on the corner of Walker and Cooper streets in Redfern, I would catch the train from Pendle Hill to the city each morning, call on architects and builders during the day, and return home by train in the evening, often falling asleep and waking at the end of the line at Penrith.

When our children were young, times were tough. Marie was working long hours building up her practice, and I was trying to establish my business. We were both starting out at the same time. We couldn't even afford a septic tank for our home! Although it was a battle, there were many good days, and the people of Pendle Hill were wonderful. We still have friends living there. The children went to Girraween Public School, where Michael took to sport in a big way. His reflex ball sense was excellent. I was very careful not to put any pressure on him, however.

(In later years, when he attended Shore School (SCEGS) in North Sydney, Michael was constantly asked, 'Are you going to play rugby, like your dad?' This puts tremendous pressure on children. While I followed his progress and watched him play, I made a point of saying to him, 'Do your own thing. If you want to play the violin or the piano instead of sport, then do it and enjoy it.' As it turned out, he played in all the A-grade teams as a front-row forward and was one of the mainstays of the school's first fifteen. On leaving school he attended an agricultural college near Newcastle and played rugby in Scone, in country New South Wales. Subsequently, when he moved back to Sydney, he was the understudy to Test prop Topo Rodriguez, and played many games in the Warringah first-grade side. Overall, he was too light to play any representative football — a few extra kilograms and he probably would have made it!) He has extremely good ball sense.

Susan and Alexandra never took very much to any sport; maybe some of my grandchildren will find they have a talent in that area.

It was many months after I set up my business before I received my first order. I was fortunate that George had started a dry-cleaning business in Cleveland Street, which was around the corner from my office, so that I could transfer my phone calls to him when I wasn't in. It was a real one-man show. When my phone rang, I would answer, 'Nicholas Shehadie Pty Ltd.' When the caller asked for the accounts department or the sales department, I would pretend to transfer the call to the department they had requested. I used to get friends over to help me unload tiles from the manufacturer's trucks, as the manufacturer used to deliver them to the building sites.

My first flooring job was the bar at the New South Wales Rugby Club in Crane Place, near Circular Quay. Later, Bert Budge, who was at Wormald when I was there and later joined the engineering company Guest Keen and Nettlefold Pty Ltd (GKN) as divisional manager, asked me if I could make a computer floor panel. I said 'certainly', not having the faintest idea what he meant. The job turned out to be flooring the room that housed the mainframe computer hardware with anti-static tiles.

My Wormald training had taught me to read a plan. I measured the requirements, GKN delivered the panels, and all I had to do then was fix the tiles. As it turned out, it wasn't as simple as that: it was a new product and was still being researched. There was a violent reaction between the adhesive and the aluminium panels, which caused the tiles to lift and bubble. Luckily, GKN were most sympathetic and stood by me and helped me to solve the problem. With the assistance of the chemists at CSR, and my practical experience, we developed a formula that was to prove most successful. CSR never revealed the formula to others.

From time to time I received orders for computer floors from GKN and had to find people to assist me. I had a few fellows who were prepared to work in my mother's garage at Randwick at night and on weekends in order to complete these orders. I couldn't afford to take on full-time staff.

I managed to secure a contract to tile a Millers Hotel, run by Millers Brewery, from architects Van Breda and Vaughan, who did most of Millers' club and hotel design work. They were quite happy with our work. Foss Van Breda was a fine man and a rugby fan, and he was a tremendous help to me while I was getting my business established.

The business started to grow and I convinced my brother to close his dry-cleaning business and join me. I knew that I wouldn't be able to keep up on my own. George could see the potential, so he didn't need much persuading. We moved into premises in Elizabeth Street, Redfern, around the corner from where I had started.

We soon became the leaders in computer floors, and covered the floors of the computer rooms of most satellite tracking stations around Australia with our panels. GKN began to give us other work in scaffolding and formwork, and we soon outgrew our Elizabeth Street premises. GKN had a factory in Lewisham for sale, so I went to see the president of the then Rural Bank, Jack Fletcher, and he agreed to a reasonable loan.

At the time, GKN was one of the biggest engineering companies in the world. The new manager in Australia was an Englishman, Ron Haste. He suggested that we probably should have a contract to put our relationship on a more formal footing. We met with our lawyers, who proceeded to make things very difficult. Ron and I agreed instead to seal our 'contract' with a handshake and a beer or two. 'Let's trust each other,' we said, and the relationship was to last nearly forty years.

The factory at Lewisham became highly computerised, with robots and role formers, and with a great staff. Soon we were diversifying into the manufacture of cable ladders, as well as other similar products. With GKN doing the selling and us manufacturing, and with quite a few export orders, George took over management control of our business, which allowed me the freedom to become involved in other business, civic and sporting activities. We were — and still are — partners, and we still own the factory buildings.

* * *

My retirement from rugby left a huge gap in my life. I decided to take up refereeing, which would allow me to put something back into the game. My first task was to pass my referee's examination, which I thought would be a soft snap after playing thirty Tests, a shoal of New South Wales state appearances and around 175 first-grade games for Randwick. And, yes, I knew all the rules of the game.

I promptly failed my exam! One of the questions asked what I would do if there was a scrum on my own goal line and the full-back kicked the ball to one of my own team standing underneath the opposition's goalposts. I thought it was a ridiculous question so I gave a ridiculous answer. A second question asked what I would do if the ball being kicked for goal became deflated during its passage and finished suspended on the crossbar. 'Faint, I think,' I replied.

I got my ticket on my second attempt, and I proceeded to travel all over Sydney refereeing junior matches and, later, third- and fourth-grade club games.

One Saturday I refereed a third-grade game between St George and Eastwood at Hurstville Oval. After showering, I was enjoying a few drinks and a chat in the dressing room with some old mates. The first-grade game was in progress when the referee, Ray Priol, pulled a muscle and couldn't continue. I was called up to take over because the reserve-grade referee had already left the ground. What an experience! A good friend of mine, Alan Cameron, was captain of St George. He was well-known for arguing with referees. I took the field and promptly called Alan and another of my old

Wallaby team-mates, Ed Stapleton, who was also on the St George team, across and blew the whistle for a penalty against St George. 'What was that for?' Alan demanded. I replied that I just wanted to let him know that I was the referee and would take no nonsense from him or any of his team. I was back refereeing third grade the following week.

One time I was refereeing a third-grade game between Sydney University and Drummoyne at University Oval. The University had called on Max Elliott, a former Wallaby Test prop, to fill in by playing on the side of the scrum for the game. The prop from Drummoyne playing on the same side as Max was ruining the scrum with his antics. During a break in play, I called Max over and urged him to give this fellow a 'whack' to straighten him up. Max looked at me and I nodded. He went back and hit the Drummoyne player and they both finished up on the ground with Max coming off worst in the scuffle. He came over to me and complained, 'Didn't you see that guy hitting me?' I said, 'Yes, but you hit him first.'

After a couple of years I hung up my referee's whistle and was appointed both a New South Wales and Australian selector. I enjoyed my time as a selector. I felt that I understood the game. I prided myself on being able to concentrate on one particular player for ten minutes at a time, a technique I had learned from Wally Meagher. I could also read a scrum very well — the placement of the feet and necks of the front-row props, which revealed who was and who wasn't packing correctly. Scrummaging often produced differences of opinion and long discussions among the selectors.

Once a team was selected, it became the team chosen by all the selectors, but one argument that I put forward, and which won the day after a long debate, concerned John Thornett, who appeared likely to miss out in the New South Wales team as a back-row forward. I felt he was much too good a player to leave out, although he had slowed up a little. I was convinced he had the ideal build to play in the front row, and the intelligence and background to adapt in that position. It took some time to convince my co-selectors, but they finally agreed and John went on to be a great front-rower in many Test matches.

Tony Miller was another player I had a big input in moving to the front row from his regular spot in the second row with some lineout responsibilities. Players such as Thornett and Miller might have been slowing up, but they still had plenty to offer and their experience and enthusiasm would benefit any team.

On one occasion, in the early sixties, we had selected a Test team to meet New Zealand in Brisbane and we didn't have a single Queenslander in the line-up. The selectors came in for a great deal of booing and hissing on their arrival at the ground, and when we were shown to our seats we found that we had been placed behind some posts! Queenslanders are great folks, but boy, are they parochial!

A young half-back by the name of Ken Catchpole had just broken through the ranks and, playing for New South Wales against the British Lions in 1959, played a blinder. I had seen a great deal of Ken from his days at Randwick, both in the juniors as well as the senior teams, and Wally Meagher had followed his progress in school football with the Scots College. He, no doubt, was the greatest prospect in Australian rugby at that time. He was up against another great half-back from Queensland for selection in the Wallabies, the tried-and-tested Des Connor, who held the Australian Test position that year before moving off to New Zealand where he won selection with the All Blacks. Catchpole is probably the best half-back I have seen; there was simply nothing he couldn't do. It was a tragic day for rugby in 1968 when, playing against New Zealand at the Sydney Cricket Ground, Colin Meads was involved in an incident which badly injured Catchpole and ended his career. He later joined me on the Sydney Cricket Ground Trust, and it was a privilege to work with him.

I derived great satisfaction from my time as a selector, particularly watching players who later went on to do great things. I eventually broke away from rugby in 1962 after serving my three-year selector's stint. It was at around this time that I was approached to join the Council of the City of Sydney.

Part Two

A PUBLIC LIFE

10 ENTERING POLITICS

I can honestly say that a career in politics had never entered my mind until Walter Spooner, the then director of the Civic Reform Association, a non-aligned ratepayers' association, contacted me and suggested that I stand as an alderman for the council elections of the City of Sydney. They were looking for candidates, and I was in no doubt that they wanted to capitalise on my sporting experience and profile — the Shehadies were well known in the Redfern area.

I wasn't associated with any political party, but after several meetings with Spooner, and having been reassured that there was no political party affiliation, I realised there was some merit in these discussions and that perhaps I could make some sort of contribution to my community. I was always looking for challenges, and this one appealed to me. I was also opposed to politics in local government, because local issues such as garbage collection don't need to be politicised — they just need to be done efficiently. I had a slight acquaintance with Harry Jensen, the then Labor lord mayor, from his days as a patron of my football club when he was mayor of Randwick. (The mayor of Randwick was always the patron of the Randwick Rugby Football Club.) Jensen was a prominent figure who came from the Coogee area; he later became a minister in the state government. That was all I knew about the city council.

At the time we were living in Pendle Hill and life was busy, with me establishing the tiling business and Marie working in her practice and studying to become a psychiatrist, but she agreed to support me. In 1962 I stood as a Civic Reform candidate in the Northcott Ward, which covered the areas of Redfern, Waterloo, Alexandria, Rosebery, Newtown, Camperdown and Enmore. There were four wards comprising the city boundaries, and five aldermen to be elected from each ward. The city council covered a far bigger area then than it does now — when I first entered the council it covered all of what is now South Sydney Council.

Having had a lifelong connection with Redfern, I suppose it was a natural step for me to represent the area on the city council. It was going to be hard competing against the Labor team, but I saw the challenge and my ego got the better of me. Even before my business had moved to the Lewisham factory, a brick was thrown through my office window in Redfern. 'Welcome to local government!' I thought, and capitalised on the publicity. This incident only made me more determined to win a seat, although I was up against the Australian Labor Party (ALP) machine with such tough opponents as Cliff Noble, Harry Burland, Tom Foster and Mick Ibbett. Ernie O'Dea and Con Wallace, who represented other wards, were in control of the council — these were the big boys in the ALP machine. It was a culture shock, coming in from the cold and never having been involved in politics. I was elected with the other four gentlemen.

What an experience! Council meetings were quite an education. When the poll was declared in the Sydney Town Hall, Cec Kyle, the leader of the Civic Reform Association, let fly with a tirade of accusations against the Labor Party about rorting during the election. Then the lord mayor, Harry Jensen, got up and had a go back at the Civic Reform group. Then all hell broke loose. People were screaming insults. I was standing alongside a fellow of about my age who said it was his first experience, too, and he was also shocked. He turned out to be ALP alderman Tony Bradford, who represented the Rocks area, and although we were on opposite sides, we became very good friends.

I was in for what turned out to be a traumatic learning experience with men like Ernie O'Dea, Con Wallace, Gil Roper, Cliff Noble, Mick Ibbett and Reg Murphy, all tough nuts from the ALP. Civic Reform had a few guys who could match them, including Emmet McDermott, David Griffin, Bill Northam, Graham Nock and Cec Kyle. I became a member of the committee responsible for development applications, and of the Health Committee responsible for garbage collection, parks and gardens, the medical and dental clinic, and the libraries. The staff were extremely professional, and many of them took me under their wing. Being in opposition, one cannot achieve much, especially when the ALP have caucused — they would meet before each meeting to decide how to vote. We could win every argument but lose every vote. Nevertheless, I enjoyed the rough and tumble of life as an alderman.

In my role as alderman, I learned much from Cliff Noble, who was the senior member among the ALP. He was always polite and fair in his dealings with me, and he was a very good deputy lord mayor. I was young, raw and eager to learn, and at times quite naive about the complex world of politics. I wasn't afraid to have a go, though — which in hindsight helped gain me a good standing. Ernie O'Dea used to say to me, 'Son, *I'll* teach you …!' I was often cheeky and was once thrown out of a meeting for interjecting when Alderman Gil Roper got up to ask a question about prostitution in a local premises and about VD being on the increase at those premises. I couldn't contain myself, calling out, 'But you're cured now, aren't you?' Lord Mayor Harry Jensen said, 'Retract that statement!' I called out, 'I want to see his health certificate!' The place was in an uproar. Harry was laughing, but he ordered me out of the chamber.

I got on very well with the Labor boys, although we had some great differences of opinion. They'd have a go at me, and I was bold enough to have a go back. I had sympathy for the Party, heavily influenced by my boyhood respect for Bill McKell, a family friend.

Con Wallace was the master politician, despite having suffered a stroke. He led the whole group. To get anything done on the council, you had to have Con on side. He was very bright. He could debate you on any subject, plucking numbers from the air and sounding most authoritative. He was the leader of a team that included Harry Jensen, who later became a state government minister. Sitting opposite Con in council I learned much that would assist me in the years to come. He hardened me and taught me to understand a little more about politics. Although we clashed a number of times, I liked the man and I am pleased we became good friends. He was reputed to be one of the owners of the Hasty Tasty Club at Kings Cross. I recall when we would make inspections of properties prior to making decisions on development applications. On one particular occasion, Con hobbled up the steps of an elderly woman's terrace house with us trailing behind him. He cheekily introduced himself as 'Alderman David Griffin of the Civic Reform' and announced that he 'could not possibly approve this application'. That was prior to the election, of course!

Having come from the world of football, I found the world of politics all very exciting.

During this period, Marie and I moved our family from Pendle Hill back closer to the city. Marie's psychiatry course was for three years, during some of which time she had to live in at Callan Park, in the inner-western suburb of Rozelle. Life was full-on, and it made sense to live nearer the university and Marie's live-in quarters.

We looked around for a home but couldn't afford many places, so we stayed for a time with Marie's brother, Sam, in Coogee, before finding at last a place that we could afford in Mosman.

During my second term in 1966 I became more active in our team and was elected deputy leader to Emmet McDermott. I was happy to take on more responsibility. Life continued in its hectic way — I was running my business as well as attending to council matters — but I was enjoying the fast pace. John Armstrong, the former federal Labor senator, became lord mayor and later Australia's high commissioner in London. John, like Harry Jensen, was a man of great integrity and was highly respected. He was known as 'the Golden Barman' because he owned lots of hotels and was reputed to be very wealthy. This was around the time that

In 1972, in my earlier role as deputy lord mayor, I escorted Prince Charles out onto George Street in Sydney's business centre, where he happily chatted with enthusiastic citizens.

Graham Nock introduced me to sailing. However, Bill Northam, an Olympic sailing representative in his day, didn't join us during our second term. The state government had changed during this period, with Liberal Bob Askin becoming premier and Pat Morton the minister for local government.

It was decided that the boundaries of the city council should be redistributed and some changes made. The whole of my ward was to become South Sydney. In 1967 we were all dismissed overnight without warning, and three commissioners were appointed while the government examined the projected boundary alterations. It was all very political. It had happened to past councils, but it still came as a shock. It wasn't a pleasant feeling to be informed, 'You're out.' We had a good farewell party that evening, with everyone patting each other on the back in consolation. We weren't allowed back into the Town Hall after that.

The commissioners — Sir Vernon Treatt (former leader of the New South Wales Liberal Party), Sir William Pettingal (then head of the Australian Gaslight Company) and John Shaw (commissioner for main roads in New South Wales) — took up their duties immediately and remained there until September 1969, when the council elections were held under the new boundary set-up. The wards were changed to City Ward, Fitzroy Ward, Philip Ward and Macquarie Ward. South Sydney Council was established, with the northern side of Cleveland Street defining the city's boundary.

The Civic Reform Association called for candidates and I applied to stand for the Macquarie Ward, which covered the area from College Street, taking in Wooloomooloo and bordering Kings Cross.

I was ready to get back to more council work. Emmet McDermott was to lead the team, and he attracted a number of new and bright candidates — prominent businessmen such as Stan Owens, Lyn Arnold, Carr Hordern, John Harris, Andrew Briger, Joan Pilone, Leo Port, Wal Pascoe, Barry Lewis, as well as David Griffin and myself. Election day soon arrived and we had won government by twelve votes to eight. We elected Emmet unopposed as lord mayor of Sydney, and I was chosen his deputy. David Griffin became chairman of finance, an important position, and I led our team on the remaining committees.

It was decided that a strategic plan of Sydney should be our first priority. Sydney had never been planned since Captain Arthur Phillip set foot on the site nearly 200 years before. A committee of three was duly appointed to see this through, with Leo Port, an engineer, and Andrew Briger, an architect, leading the team; I was there to keep the peace if problems arose. (I like solving problems, and I seem to thrive when under pressure.) I learned a lot from both Andrew and Leo.

The three of us were very passionate about the development of Sydney. Andrew's vision was to make William Street into the Champs-Élysées of Sydney. At the time it was mostly shabby buildings. Andrew and Leo came up with the idea, Council agreed and the architecture firm of Clarke Gazzard was appointed together with Professor Peter Johnson of Sydney University's Department of Architecture. This was incredibly hard, intense work — a difficult and delicate exercise with countless hours spent deciding the model to approve. Many models were presented and debated. At times the meetings became quite heated, and both Andrew and Leo took the brunt of all this. Not only did we have to consult the public, but we had to convince our own team before presenting the final plan to council. It took nearly eighteen months of dedicated work.

From the plan, Martin Place Plaza was created, together with the William Street boulevard set-backs — buildings were set back from the road to provide more footpath space for pedestrians and outdoor eating. The then premier, Robert Askin, wasn't happy with the Martin Place plans — he thought the mall would disrupt the city traffic. Tom Lewis, then minister for lands, who was in control of such planning, suggested that we set up some bollards in Martin Place between Pitt and George streets. We made sure the bollards couldn't be removed. We knew it would work, because we had done our homework in the form of traffic control studies. We had also spent time investigating cities overseas — I had spent a week with the San Francisco planning department observing their systems.

The system to transfer site ratios was also introduced, whereby owners of historic buildings would no longer be penalised because they weren't able to develop the building. If a building was three storeys high and the legal limit was eight storeys, they could sell the extra five storeys to developers in return for maintaining and preserving the historic building. This was a pioneering decision. The first to take advantage of this new scheme was the Great Synagogue in Elizabeth Street. It was a great learning curve for me, and Sydney owes much to Andrew and Leo for their wonderful contribution. This plan is now updated every year.

In 1972, after having served three years as lord mayor, Emmet decided he didn't wish to seek a further term in office. Both he and I discussed my taking over from him, as I had been his deputy for the past three years and we had a good working relationship. We had two years to run in that term, having been re-elected in September 1971. The lord mayorship was a yearly appointment. Emmet asked me to discuss this with my fellow Civic Reform team-mate, David Griffin, who was also a frontrunner and who had performed an excellent job as finance chairman. David was also keen to take over, so we agreed that we should take on the job a year about — me first, then David the following year, which was an election year. This arrangement suited me, as I had my life organised so that I could spare the time: my brother was running my business, and it would be an easy transition from being deputy lord mayor.

Norman Barraclough, one of our senior aldermen, was privy to this discussion. But then a hiccup occurred. About a week after we'd come to our agreement, Emmet told me that I'd better have another talk to David, and that we could use his office. David informed me in that discussion that he had been instructed by the Civic Reform executive that he should be the candidate.

This development shocked me, as I had thought we had come to an arrangement. I said to him, 'Well, I'm ready to take over. What are *you* going to do?'

He said he planned to run as a candidate. At the time, he was president of the Union Club, one of the most exclusive clubs in the city, and his election would complement the business sector of the town. I suggested that perhaps I should withdraw, and he agreed. Then I said no, I wouldn't give the Civic Reform executive the satisfaction. I would run. I was angry, but didn't let it show.

I later learned that my having a non-Anglo-Saxon background didn't assist my candidature. Being Lebanese, it had occasionally been hard for me to break through barriers in Australian society, but I had never before experienced this kind of prejudice. It hurt me greatly. However, the high-profile and respected businessmen Sir John O'Neal and John Utz stood by me. That year I was beaten by a draw from a hat, but later, yes, I did become lord mayor, then deputy chief commissioner of the City of Sydney (after the previous council was sacked), and at the time I had great satisfaction in looking those people straight in the eye when I saw them next.

Sadly, Walter Spooner had now retired. I had enjoyed working with him immensely — I greatly respected him; he was like a father figure. Alex Simpson took over as chief executive of Civic Reform. I knew I had support from six of our twelve-man team, and Emmet as lord mayor would have the casting vote — I would gain the seven votes I needed.

However, the Civic Reform executive changed the rules and took the casting vote away from Emmet, which was both unpleasant and unprecedented. The voting was by exhaustive ballot and there were four nominations. John Harris was first to be eliminated, and his vote later went to David. I had received six votes but needed seven for a majority. Stan Owens went next and, like Harris, his vote went to David, leaving us six-all after three occasions. It was then decided to have a draw out of a hat. First name out would win, and it was

David's. I felt it was unfair, but I had to go along with it. Although disappointed and hurt, I wasn't going to give anyone the pleasure of seeing my true feelings. I didn't blame David — I felt he was forced to fall in with what the executive wanted.

So, David, a prominent lawyer and businessman, became lord mayor of Sydney. It was now time to elect the deputy lord mayor. I was urged to run against Joan Pilone, who was David's running mate, and I won on the first ballot.

I decided that I would see my term out, then retire quietly and gracefully. Although I stayed with the Civic Reform group, I had no confidence in some of the people at head office — there had been a lot of backroom interference by these people who weren't elected members. I had only joined them because I was assured that we would experience no outside influence. The media reported me fairly — I had always had a great relationship with the media — and Bob Askin, the premier, went on radio to publicly state that the wrong man had been appointed to the job. (I was to pay later for that remark, and Bob received a great deal of criticism for it from the business sector.)

David did the job his way and, while I supported him one hundred per cent, like some members of the Civic Reform team I didn't always agree with his approach. He was different from Emmet. He was a very proper man, highly dignified, and an intellectual. He made an official visit to Moscow, having been invited by the chairman of the Moscow Soviet, and took with him Leo Port, then chairman of the Works Committee, architect Andrew Briger, and Wal Pascoe, the team secretary, as well as the lord mayor's private secretary, David Taylor. When they met up upon arrival, we were later informed, the conservative Griffin had worn the lord mayor's regalia and had been mistaken for an archbishop. Wal was introduced as the party secretary, a prestigious position within the USSR, so he was treated as the boss and received most of the attention. The flamboyant Leo Port, who had stopped over in Israel on the flight, was handing out religious medallions from Israel to any Jewish people he met — which made Andrew Briger very nervous, because he wanted to avoid offending our hosts.

About mid-year 1973, on a Sunday evening at around 8.30 p.m., I received a phone call at our home in Mosman from the premier Bob Askin, asking to see me that same evening in Parliament House. He wouldn't tell me what it was about, but it sounded important. He arranged to have me picked up. On my arrival at Parliament House I was taken to Bob's office, where several people were waiting, including MPs Eric Willis and Tom Lewis. After the pleasantries, Bob sat me down and said that Nigel Bowen, the former federal minister and member for Parramatta, was going to step down and that they wanted me to take his seat. Me in Parliament? How ridiculous, I thought! I protested that I wasn't even a member of the Liberal Party. Askin assured me that that didn't matter, and he reminded me that he had put his neck out when he declared his support of me when I lost the lord mayor draw-out-of-the-hat episode. Having moved out of the Parramatta area several years earlier, I said to the premier, 'Why me?' He replied that I, as the former president of the

Parramatta Rugby Club and foundation president of its licensed club, and the son of a clergyman (the Parramatta electorate was known to have a bible belt), was 'ideal'. He assured me that I would win well and that he would call a quick state election. Gough Whitlam was prime minister and Billy Snedden was leader of the opposition.

The story broke in the press shortly after, headed '*Askin Supports Shehadie*'. Then another article appeared: '*Snedden Supports Ruddock*'. I was forced into a corner and couldn't get out. I hated the idea of not being in control of my own life, but there was nothing to be done. Marie wasn't overjoyed about the situation — this just wasn't the sort of life we wanted to lead.

Philip Ruddock was a prominent young Liberal and he had lots of backing. I wouldn't go canvassing the fifty delegates we were to appear before — it wasn't my style to do all this kind of glad-handing. However, I visited Dr Jefferies, president of the Liberal branch in that area, to pay him the respect of telling him that I was standing. He wished me every success, then informed me that his son was a candidate. Everyone was coaching me on policies, foreign affairs and the economy, and even a dear friend, Robin Lovejoy, the then head of the National Institute for the Dramatic Arts, coached me on the arts. I was getting so much advice from so many people, I was becoming confused.

The day came when more than thirty of us appeared before the preselectors at the then Wentworth Hotel in Sydney. Each of us addressed the gathering, then answered questions from the floor. Philip Ruddock's supporters gave me a tough time, but I didn't mind.

My speech was on urban development. Then, late in the evening, we were reduced to the last five candidates and we each had to make a further speech and answer more questions. It was gruelling, but I was happy to work hard and try my best.

At 11 p.m. the announcement was made that Philip Ruddock had won. I was informed that he had received twenty-five votes, I had got twenty-four, and that there had been one informal vote. I had done my best — I lost to a very fine man. I got to know Philip Ruddock quite well after that encounter and hold him in high regard.

I rang Marie, who picked me up from the hotel. We went to a friend's house where he and I shared a bottle of Scotch. I had paid my dues. The next morning I left home and spent the day at Fred Allsop's racing stables at Randwick, where I was part-owner of a thoroughbred. I felt completely washed out. I sat and fed the horse a carrot while reflecting on recent events. The news that evening announced that I had gone away to the Central Coast and couldn't be contacted.

On the Monday, the lord mayoral election was scheduled, and I didn't want to stand. I felt that I had had my time. I had been defeated once already, and it was just the right time to slip out of public life. It was rumoured that there would be several candidates and that David Griffin would lose. When I arrived home from the stables, Marie had a bunch of messages for me, including a strong request from my team that I stand for lord mayor. I didn't return any of the calls. I purposely arrived late for the team meeting that day so as to avoid any prior discussion that might involve me. I felt completely drained.

To my surprise, I was confronted by several of my colleagues pressuring me to throw my hat into the ring; they said that if *I* didn't, others would. I felt very confused. The meeting commenced and David called for nominations. As one nominated oneself, David then nominated himself. I was getting glances from around the table, even the odd kick in the shin, so on the third call I said, 'Put up the name Shehadie.' My thoughts had focused on the fact that David was losing support and was so out of touch that he didn't realise he was losing it.

Norman Barraclough and Carr Hordern were elected as scrutineers, and we placed our votes into a clean wastepaper container. It wasn't pleasant sitting in the room, especially when David, I'm sure, didn't think he would be opposed. It didn't take long to get the result: ten to two in my favour. I thanked David for his contribution and the others for their support. David left the room, bitterly disappointed. Having been in that position myself a year earlier, I fully understood his feelings.

As I mentioned earlier, the position was up for grabs: many people were planning to nominate. Marie knew nothing of this and, to my surprise, she later arrived at the Town Hall, feeling, I think, more embarrassed than excited. I later learned that Norman Barraclough, unbeknown to me, had sent a car to pick her up. It was all such a surprise; we weren't really prepared for it.

I was to take over in a week's time as lord mayor. It wasn't good timing for me, as my brother was overseas for a month and I was running the business. Ron Haste, the managing director of GKN, the British engineering company for whom we manufactured, sent me a helper until George returned. It was a hectic few days: I had lost a preselection for Canberra and become Sydney's lord mayor.

Friends rallied around me. Within a few weeks, as part of my duties as lord mayor, Marie and I had to arrange the Lady Mayoress's Ball. The ball was an annual fixture on the city's social calendar, but this one would coincide with the opening of Sydney's now famous Opera House. Leading identities such as John Laws, Robin Lovejoy and Stephen Hall, head of the Australian Opera at the time, were most helpful in planning the occasion. Marie excelled at organising the festivities. She had had some experience of organising balls and functions when she was at Women's College at Sydney University, and she went about doing the job with her usual grace and efficiency. Soon all the tickets had sold out — which was unprecedented for the event — and a substantial sum was raised for the Lady Mayoress's fundraising committee charities.

It was a marvellous night. The governor, the late Sir Roden Cutler, and Lady Cutler were the guests of honour; the Navy band played; dancing was in the beautiful vestibule — Marie's idea, which worked perfectly; and dinner was served in the main hall. Every senior rugby club in Sydney booked a table in support of me, and every room in the Town Hall was the scene of a party. The last of the guests didn't leave until 5 a.m.

The staff did a tremendous job and had the Town Hall spick and span for the 9 a.m. opening the next day of the Waratah Festival. They were fine, dedicated, supportive people. It was a great way to start my first term as lord mayor.

A long way from my rugged boyhood Redfern days: lord mayor of Sydney in all the regalia plus the weighty chain.

Usually, before going to the Town Hall to begin my day in my public capacity, I would call in at our factory in Lewisham to have a talk with George and the staff. On one particular morning, Des Hanley, my driver, arrived to collect me from home at 7.30 a.m. in the lord mayor's official vehicle, a Rolls-Royce. We gave Marie a lift to her workplace at Broughton Hall, in Rozelle, as her car was off the road for the day. After dropping her off, I remained in the back seat as we proceeded through Leichhardt on the way to the factory. At around 8 a.m. we were in a line of traffic crossing an intersection when a car, travelling at considerable speed down a slight hill, failed to stop and give way to the right. It slammed into the front passenger side of our car, forcing it into the lane of oncoming traffic. The impact wrote off both the errant driver's car and one of the oncoming vehicles. The damage to the Rolls was bad enough, and I'm sure that, had we been travelling in a less sturdy vehicle, we would have suffered serious injury.

Des had only just washed and polished the car and was so upset I thought he was going to attack the driver, who didn't seem at all concerned about his own vehicle, probably because it belonged to his boss. The local residents had long been trying to have a stop sign installed at that intersection, and I smile to myself nowadays when I pass the intersection and see the sign. It didn't take long for the media to inform all of Australia that I had been in an accident, and I received many interstate calls congratulating me on my lucky escape. I have loved Rolls-Royces ever since that day!

Princess Anne steps out on her honeymoon visit to Sydney after her marriage to Captain Mark Phillips. She is an enthusiastic rugby supporter who certainly takes the game seriously, serving as patron of the Scottish Rugby Union and reportedly never missing a match.

Preparing for the official opening of the Opera House was an exciting time. I was on the committee headed by Sir Asher Joel. It was a one-man show — he was a brilliant organiser.

The opening was a day to remember. Her Majesty Queen Elizabeth II and Prince Philip, together with other members of the royal family, had come to Sydney for the occasion, along with many other world leaders. The city was beautifully decorated. Marie and I took up our positions on the Opera House steps with Her Majesty when she officially opened the building. That evening, the orchestral concert conducted by Sir Charles Mackerras and featuring the great Swedish Wagnerian soprano Birgit Nilsson was magnificent.

During my term I had the privilege of meeting many interesting people. I had previously met the Queen in 1948 on our Wallaby tour when she was Princess Elizabeth, and King George VI and the then Queen hosted us at Buckingham Palace. Lord Halsham was another notable visitor, as were a number of popular entertainers, including Danny Kaye, Carol Burnett, Tim Conway and Lee Marvin, plus heads of state and various sporting teams.

During my term I experienced many changes in Sydney, such as the development of the Woolloomooloo basin. Running along the waterfront between Kings Cross and the city, it was the site of the wharves for all the big ships that used the harbour. Overdevelopment of the area was becoming a problem. Victoria Street, Potts Point, with its rows of terraces overlooking the harbour, was in danger of being torn down and redeveloped. One of the biggest problems I faced was the green bans, where workers downed their tools in protest at the destruction of Sydney's heritage buildings and low-income housing. There were green bans on all of Woolloomooloo. It was a tough time. My sympathies were with the locals, but I had to operate within the law. At times the law wasn't in the best interests of our future, and on many occasions we had to act on the side of the developers, who were working within the guidelines as prescribed at the time.

There were weekly meetings with Jack Mundey, then head of the New South Wales Builders' Labourers' Federation (BLF), who was the leader of the famous protests. I always felt that Jack was sincere and deserved much credit for his stand on the preservation of the terraces.

Juanita Nielsen, who ran a local newspaper called *Now*, was extremely vocal about the proposed development. Attending most council meetings, she would report the activities of council, opposing many of its decisions. I always found her to be a very pleasant person who was passionate about her beloved Kings Cross. Mysteriously, she suddenly disappeared and her body has never been found.

Many months later, Norm Gallagher, the infamous federal president of the BLF from Victoria, came to see me. He took over the BLF in New South Wales, ousting Jack Mundey, and things were getting pretty rough. I would never see developers, or anyone involved in developments, on my own — I always had someone from council with me. On this occasion, Andrew Briger was with me. Norm, a big man wearing a cardigan, walked into my office with one of his representatives. I'd never met him before.

'G'day, Nick,' he said.

'G'day, Norm,' I replied.

I introduced him to Andrew and asked, 'What can I do for you?' He told me he wanted the bans lifted from some of the buildings in Woolloomooloo.

'It's not on,' I said. 'I'm not interested. It's got to be all or nothing.' He told me that he was going to write to me about releasing the green bans from some of the buildings.

'I'm not going to reply,' I said, which I followed with: 'Would you like a drink?'

Norm had a whisky, then a few more. When he left, he announced again that he was going to write to me to say that he was lifting the ban from one building. I maintained my stance that I wouldn't reply to any letter from him. (I think the whisky was a great help at the time.) In a few weeks I received a call from Gallagher's office saying that he wanted to come in and see me. I decided that I wasn't going to jump at his every command, so I made the appointment a week or so later. He walked in, and again I was with Andrew.

'G'day, Nick,' he said.

'G'day, Norm.'

'Are you going to offer me a drink?' he asked.

I said, 'No, I want to hear what you have to say.'

'I'm lifting the bans from the lot.'

'Have a drink,' I said.

The green bans in Woolloomooloo were over. This was a great break through in the history of Sydney.

In my mind, one of the most important successes I enjoyed was to bring together the three levels of government needed to take charge of the redevelopment of Woolloomooloo: the federal prime minister, Gough Whitlam (Labor); the state premier, Tom Lewis (Liberal); and myself as lord mayor. We signed an agreement to cooperate, and it worked. We formed the Woolloomooloo Planning Committee, which I chaired. It took over a year to complete the redevelopment plan. Regular meetings took place, with Tom Uren, minister for urban and regional development (representing the federal government), Sir John Fuller, minister for planning (representing the state government). The planners did a marvellous job. They worked day and night, talking with local people in the area. The beautiful terraces of Victoria Street were preserved.

Sydney was experiencing great changes. More people were being attracted back into the city from the suburbs, pedestrian plazas made it a whole lot easier to get around, and building set-backs were working. People loved the wider footpaths. We guaranteed the preservation of the classic old Queen Victoria Building, and we encouraged many outdoor concerts. I even had a Lord Mayor's 'jazzmobile' that played in various locations on Saturdays. I believed in getting the business sector financially involved. I had lots of friends and contacts who were happy to help by funding things like the jazzmobile.

I also wanted to change the Waratah Festival. With its floats, bands and marching girls, I felt it wasn't right for Sydney. Sydney could do better. I discussed this with Sir Asher Joel, always affectionately known as 'Mr Sydney'. (Whatever event was being planned in Sydney at the time — the official opening of the Opera House, say, or the visit of Pope Paul VI — Sir Asher would be in charge of it.)

With Asher Joel's help, I engaged Stephen Hall, who was then a producer with the Australian Opera, guaranteeing him three years' salary, paid for by private enterprise. With Sir Asher, I approached the premier, Tom Lewis, and asked for $50 000 towards establishing the Festival of Sydney. He just laughed at me. Sir Asher said, 'Tell him what you want it for, first!' After much discussion, the premier approved the request.

With the blessing of the state government, the Festival of Sydney was established in 1975 in the place of the Waratah Festival. From its small beginnings, it has gone from strength to strength. Initially it was a week-long celebration showcasing various cultural activities. After a time it became a month-long festival. Now it is a major cultural event in Sydney, held each January.

One highlight of my lord-mayoral term was the visit to Sydney in 1974 of Sir Murray Fox, the lord mayor of London, who arrived with his entourage, including his sheriff, sword bearer and footmen. His visit coincided with the annual Lady Mayoress's Ball. The Town Hall was packed with people and was beautifully decorated in a half-London/half-Sydney theme. Murray led his group in full regalia down the centre of the hall to the tune of 'Rule Britannia', and I led our aldermen. I had arranged for the students at my son's school to be dressed in blue and red, and they all stood on the Town Hall steps greeting

FAIRFAX PHOTO LIBRARY

Smiles to greet Sydney. In 1974 this joyous moment involved a visiting children's choir from Korea joining me on the balcony of the Sydney Town Hall.

the crowds while bands played on the footpath outside. It was a spectacular, grand occasion.

In 1975 I made a formal visit to London at the invitation of Sir Murray Fox. I was accompanied by David Taylor, my private secretary, and Marie. We stayed at Mansion House, the official residence of the lord mayor of London. It was an exciting visit. I was presented at the Guild Hall, and Sir Murray held several receptions in our honour.

The Australian embassy in Rome had arranged for me and Marie to have a private audience with His Holiness, Pope Paul VI, on our way to London. We felt both thrilled and privileged. It was a very moving experience. We had arrived in Rome via Hong Kong, where Marie had been waiting for me in the transit lounge. She had spent the three previous weeks in China, visiting numerous medical institutions, as well as places of great cultural and historic importance. We were en route to the Iranian capital, Tehran, to meet with that city's lord mayor, who was to make an official visit to Sydney as a guest of the Australian government. Sadly, he was executed in that country's subsequent coup.

We were met on our arrival in Rome by the Australian ambassador. On the morning following our arrival, at 11 a.m., the official embassy car arrived to drive us to the Vatican. Marie was dressed in black with long sleeves and gloves, and a beautiful black veil. Arriving at St Peter's Basilica through the rear entrance gates, we couldn't help but admire the colourfully garbed Swiss guards who have stood sentry at the entrance for the last hundred or so years.

We came to the Papal apartments and were met by a member of the Vatican staff in impeccable formal dress. We were then escorted upstairs and through an elegant loggia along which were hanging priceless paintings by Raphael. We walked along the long passage to the section occupied by His Holiness. A number of anterooms came off the corridor, and we were shown to the last in the succession of rooms from which visitors are presented. My eye was caught by a magnificent-looking black African cardinal in his striking vestments.

After chatting in whispers for about thirty minutes, we were approached by the Pope's secretary, who asked us what language we would be speaking. Since our designated language was English, it wasn't necessary for us to have an interpreter, as His Holiness spoke perfect English. Our entry into the private library of Pope Paul VI was a moment of great emotion for us. We had both met His Holiness on the Town Hall steps when he had visited Sydney during my term as deputy lord mayor, and a few days later my mother had accompanied me to an ecumenical service with him, which was conducted in the Sydney Town Hall.

As my emotions quietened, I became aware of the calm beauty and magnificent dimensions of the room. It was here that His Holiness received heads of state, ministers and foreign governments in private audience. The very atmosphere pervading the room seemed to symbolise the scholarliness and sensitivity for which he was renowned. At the far end of the room stood a pair of glazed bookcases, between which was a painting of the Ascension into Heaven. High above the bookcases, and bordering on the glorious panelled ceiling, was a painted frieze that spanned the room, depicting bucolic scenes of great beauty, painted areas separated at intervals by angels and maidens in bas-relief. Between the bookcases and His Holiness's large, simple desk, some fifteen high-backed Renaissance-style chairs, upholstered in velvet, were set, as if for a conference.

His Holiness greeted us, and I was impressed by how serene and distinguished he looked, dressed in white, a gold cross on his chest, and with radiant blue eyes that welcomed us with great warmth. His Holiness expressed an informed and detailed interest in Marie's work with children, and particularly her recent visit

A memorable visit to the Vatican, where Marie and I met Pope Paul VI in a private audience in his library. He greeted us so warmly.

to China. He recalled his visit to Sydney and spoke at great length about the warm welcome he had received throughout his Australian visit. I had mentioned that I was a grandson and son of a clergyman, and I shall always remember his moving response: 'We are all children of God.'

After sitting for some time, His Holiness rose and asked about our children, then presented us both with a holy medal and one each for Michael, Susan and Alexandra. He then called me across to his desk to present a book on the Raphael paintings in the Vatican. A Vatican photographer was now called in to join us for a photo session and, needless to say, these photographs today have pride of place in our Sydney home. Having spent nearly an hour in his presence, we were the last of his visitors for that day. On returning to our hotel, I was so high with joy and excitement that I reached for the cognac bottle to settle me down. We had experienced a rare privilege and a memorable reception.

After our return from our European trip, I hosted the chairman of the Moscow Soviet and his entourage of ten. Mr Promislov was a very powerful man, one of the top five in the Russian hierarchy. He was returning David Griffin's earlier visit to the Soviet Union. He brought with him his deputy, plus the state architect. On the Saturday of his visit we took Mr Promislov out on the harbour. That day was the running of the Lord Mayor's Cup horse race at Rosehill, in Sydney's west. The boat took us along the Parramatta River and we disembarked at Concord. There was a magnificent building opposite the wharf, and the Russian architect, through the interpreter, asked what it was. No one could tell him. Later, Marie, being a person who loved history and historical buildings, checked it out. It was the historic home of Thomas Walker, a prominent early businessman and philanthropist, and in recent years had been used by the Benevolent Society, who were in the process of vacating it. When Marie learned this, she set about convincing the New South Wales government that it would be the ideal premises, with its vast grounds, for a home for teenagers with social or other problems. It is now Rivendell, the adolescent unit attached to Royal Prince Alfred Hospital.

Official cars met us at the wharf and took us to the races. There was a horse called 'Moscow' running in the Cup. A complete outsider, it ran last, and the Russians thought this had been done deliberately to embarrass them. They weren't happy at all, especially the KGB officers who were accompanying the party. All our explanations to them that the failure of the horse to perform well hadn't been planned made no difference, so we had to leave the racecourse.

In 1975, Marie had become quite ill with a neck condition and was hospitalised for many weeks after undergoing major surgery. She wore a neck brace for some time. Now in my second term as lord mayor, and having won the council election in September of that year with a majority that had increased from twelve to eight to seventeen to three, things had gone well for me, so I thought that the following September would be the right time to step down. I had done enough and I was concerned about Marie. I planned to sit on the back bench until the next general election in 1977 and then retire gracefully.

I didn't tell my team of my decision until the very last moment, so as to keep their minds on the job and thus eliminate much lobbying between my fellow aldermen. Leo Port had become my deputy during my second term, thus making him a frontrunner as next lord mayor. When the time came, I received sympathetic coverage in the press. Leo won the team support, but Andrew Briger gave him a good run for it. Leo performed a good job in planning Sydney and, sadly, he was to die in office. Andrew was deputy, but was never to become lord mayor, which was a great pity as he really deserved to earn that position, given the wonderful contribution he had made to Sydney. He later became mayor of Woollahra, a harbourside municipality.

On my retirement, I devoted myself to my business and was invited to join several company boards. My learning curve continued. One evening in 1987, almost ten years later, Pat Hills, the former state member and my chairman on the Sydney Cricket Ground Trust, rang me to say the government was about to dismiss the City of Sydney council and wanted me to become the deputy chief commissioner. My first reaction was, 'No way — been there, done that!'

Pat said that Sir Eric Neal was to be chief commissioner and the third member was to be Norm Oakes, former head of Treasury in New South Wales. Eric later rang me, saying that we should do this in the interests of Sydney, and he insisted that I join him. I had worked with Eric previously on various boards and committees, and knew him to be very capable and well-respected. He was later to become governor of South Australia. That evening, Barry Unsworth, the premier, rang to tell me that he wanted me to take on the role. I asked him when he was going to dismiss the council, and he replied, 'Tomorrow morning.'

Doug Sutherland was lord mayor, and Frank Sartor and Clover Moore were aldermen, as was Jeremy Bingham. As the commissioners, we decided to share the job three ways. Eric would look after the everyday running of things, Norman would look after the finances and welfare, and I became the commissioner responsible for development, planning and cleansing (incorporating street cleaning, garbage collection and so on), working very closely with Norman Oakes. There was a huge backlog in development applications. We advertised that we were available to meet the public on scheduled days, and we finally ran out of people to see. Certainly, no one was denied an interview.

Some of the developments we approved were Governor Phillip Tower, Chifley Square, and the construction over the Kings Cross tunnel. One development we refused to agree to was a building proposed to be erected opposite the Town Hall, on a site owned by Alan Bond's company. Bond sought permission to build a massive 102-storey complex. I would have no part in that, and we set a limit of fifty-six storeys. Another conflict I had with Bond's company was his request to implode the building where Chifley Square now stands. We couldn't gain the necessary insurance guarantees that the surrounding buildings would be safe. This sort of thing was new, and we weren't prepared to commit Sydney to such a proposal, especially as we were only caretakers.

In 1987 I was in Belgium, where Wormald had a manufacturing plant, attending a board meeting. Sir Eric Neal telephoned me. He asked if I could get to Portsmouth, in England, to be the Sydney representative to farewell the Tall Ships, which were sailing to Sydney for the bicentennial celebrations the next year, when Australia would be celebrating 200 years of European settlement of the country. I would also receive a ceremonial longboat on behalf of Sydney. I found that I could make it to Portsmouth in the stipulated time.

I arrived in London, where I was met by an old friend from GKN days, Ron Haste. We proceeded to Farnham Common, in Buckinghamshire, where I stayed with Ron and his wife Dorothy, who had already received my itinerary from Sydney. The official car was to collect me at 6.30 a.m. the following day. I had invited Dorothy to accompany me to Portsmouth. She was tremendously excited at the prospect of meeting Her Majesty Queen Elizabeth. As we left the house, to our amazement we found that several dozen Union Jacks had been stuck in the grass alongside the driveway; they had been placed there by neighbours to celebrate Dorothy's first meeting with the Royals.

After a drive of several hours, our black limousine, which was flying the City of Sydney flag (flown over for the occasion), arrived in Portsmouth. Doug McLelland, the then Australian high commissioner in London, and his wife Lorna headed the Australian delegation, accompanied by Kevin Stewart, who was the New South Wales agent-general in London.

There was a huge crowd present, and many Australian spectators.

We took our positions, and then Her Majesty and Prince Philip arrived. To our delight, a marching band of young Australians entered the area playing 'Waltzing Matilda' and looking wonderful in their bright uniforms. During a break in the proceedings, I was approached by an official of the Portsmouth council who informed me that a particular councillor would be making the presentation of the longboat to me. I refused to accept this suggestion, saying that I was the official representative of the City of Sydney and so the presentation must be made by the lord mayor of Portsmouth. I wasn't going to have Sydney downgraded in this way. The high commissioner was nearby and heard what was going on, and he totally supported my stance. The lord mayor then approached me and we had a short discussion wherein he told me that he had only been lord mayor for two days and wasn't sure of the procedure. I soon put that right and all went to plan.

We were all later presented to Her Majesty, which Dorothy enjoyed immensely. We then farewelled the Tall Ships as they commenced their long journey to Sydney, where they were due to arrive on 26 January, Australia Day, 1988.

On that day, I was seated in the forecourt of the Opera House with all the other dignitaries, headed by Her Majesty Queen Elizabeth and Prince Philip, to witness the spectacular sight of the armada of Tall Ships, surrounded by hundreds of small craft, as it reached the shores of Australia after its long voyage from England. At one function later on in the celebrations, Prince Philip asked me if I had been recycled!

Her Majesty Queen Elizabeth and Prince Philip leaving Sydney Town Hall with Marie and me prior to the opening of the Opera House in 1973.

In 1988, Nick Greiner had won the state election and was keen to restore the aldermen back at the Town Hall at an early election. The Greiner government proposed to split the City Council in two. South Sydney Council was to be established as a separate entity that would include Woolloomooloo, Kings Cross and Elizabeth Bay, in addition to areas south-west of the city, such as Newtown and Camperdown. Norm Oakes and I were responsible for setting up the staff of South Sydney Council. We suggested that Woolloomooloo, Kings Cross and Elizabeth Bay should remain within the City of Sydney boundaries. We weren't successful.

We had to move in haste, so we purchased a building in Zetland which became the head office of South Sydney Council. I interviewed all those staff for whom transferring to South Sydney was a problem, which weren't many. Both Norm and I were determined that South Sydney would be viable and be given a solid start financially, with good staff, and vehicles and machinery in first-class condition. We appointed John Bourke, an experienced public servant, as town clerk and involved him in the selection of all of his senior staff. Vic Smith, an employee of the City Council, was elected mayor. The commissioners left at the end of 1988, leaving both councils debt-free and in first-class order, with no backlogs. The council staff were very professional, particularly during this period, and did a great job.

As I look back on my days in local government, it was indeed an interesting period and I appreciate the wonderful experiences it gave me. Local government is the government that's closest to the people, because it deals with everyday issues. Sydney is a great city. I feel privileged to have been born and raised here and am proud that I have been involved in its development. I am also proud to have been known as the 'flowering lord mayor', having decorated the bases of the city's lampposts and other areas with flowerbeds, which no one had thought to do before.

11 THE SYDNEY CRICKET GROUND TRUST, 1978–2001

I guess I fell under the spell of the Sydney Cricket Ground the first day I walked through its gates. A wide-eyed young sports lover, I sensed at once its unique aura of history and tradition. It has never left me, for the SCG has been a large part of my life, initially as an enthusiastic spectator, then as a player on the famous turf, then later again as a passionately proud administrator of the ground. Each time I gaze across the rich green turf I am reminded that this was Sir Donald Bradman's favourite ground, where he paraded skills that highlighted the golden days of Australian cricket. I saw the Don make his farewell through the SCG members' gate, just as I witnessed other memorable events: the Ron Roberts try that won victory for Australia's Rugby League team against Great Britain; Tony Lockett's record-breaking goal-kicking moment; Shane Warne's capture of his 300th Test wicket; and much, much more.

I relished my early visits to the SCG as a member, seated high in the M.A. Noble grandstand with its commanding view of the wicket. Two decidedly devoted cricket enthusiasts, Marie and I would arrive with the all-important lunch basket. Indeed, we were so engrossed in the action during one Test match that our son, Michael, came close to being born in that grandstand. It needed a fairly desperate cab drive to get Marie to the hospital in time.

While I loved cricket, rugby was my chosen game. I will never forget the day when I ran out onto that field for my first rugby Test appearance against the redoubtable New Zealand All Blacks.

My travels have taken me to many parts of the world and I have visited and inspected most of the great international sporting stadiums — Wembley, Twickenham, Murrayfield, Ellis Park, Eden Park, the old Cardiff Arms Park, to name a few — but none has ever aroused in me quite the same thrill and high expectancy as the SCG does so regularly. I couldn't have envisaged in those early days that one day I would begin a 23-year stint as one of the ground's trustees and for eleven years would be its chairman.

The period from 1978 to 2001 proved to be eventful, and controversial, bringing changes that altered the whole face of the SCG. We modernised the ground with giant new grandstands, installed towering floodlights, removed the famous grass-bank 'Hill', created the adjoining Football Stadium, now the home of so much international football, and introduced the Walk of Honour. Oh, and yes — there was that acrimonious encounter with the organisers of the 2000 Olympic Games, when the SCG's future may well have been in the balance.

It was 1978 when I received a phone call from the minister of sport, Ken Booth, inviting me to become a trustee of the Sydney Cricket Ground and Sports Ground Trust. Positions on the SCG Trust were highly sought after. At the time, I was busily occupied at my factory, as well as being a committee member of the Sydney Turf Club, patron of the Randwick Rugby Club and a member of several commercial boards. I had a fair bit on, but I was happy to find the time because it was such a great privilege to be asked.

I had been a member since 1949 and had always treated my membership as an honour. The Neville Wran Labor government had put through legislation changing the format and tenure of appointments. Prior to this change, appointments were made for life, and many politicians enjoyed their positions on the Trust, including Sir William McKell, Bill Sheehan, Sir Robert Askin, Tom Lewis, Pat Hills and the then chief justice and president of Australian Rugby Union, Sir Leslie Herron, along with sportsmen such as Arnold Tancred, Mick Grace, Arthur Morris and Ian Craig. The new system would restrict appointments to two and four years, with those trustees being eligible for reappointment. The Trust membership was increased, allowing the members to have a representation of two by vote every four years. That year, 1978, Pat Hills and Arthur Morris were reappointed, while the new appointees included sports identities such as Betty Cuthbert, Kevin Humphries (Rugby League), Jim Bayutti (soccer) and myself.

Betty Cuthbert was the first woman to be appointed as a trustee. I recall her phoning me, very excited, and asking what sort of contribution she could make. I assured her that we would stick together and serve on the same committees. She turned out to be a great trustee and certainly left her mark. Pat Hills was a marvellous chairman, a fine leader who never brought politics into his decisions. The new Brewongle Stand was under construction when we were appointed, and the concrete pour of one of the floors was aborted when the men walked off the job, ruining the entire floor. Pat Hills resolved the strike with the unions, and all went well. The new lights were also being erected for the introduction of the day/night cricket promotions.

I became a member of the Works and Grounds Committee under the leadership of Arthur Morris, who was a wonderful man to work with. We supervised the development of the Churchill and O'Reilly stands and all of the necessary maintenance. Controversy raged over the demolition and disappearance of the famous 'Hill', home to many thousands of cricket and football diehards down the years, and always a vibrant and colourful scene. The great grassy bank was part of our heritage; however, crowd control, mainly during the day/night cricket games, became a major problem that could only be solved by the construction of grandstand seating. It was only after long and in-depth discussions with the New South Wales Cricket Association (NSWCA), and in the interests of public safety, that we decided we had to take this dramatic step. The decision wasn't taken lightly.

Pat Hills didn't have a very good relationship with the cricket authorities, and many a heated discussion took place between Pat and the president of the NSWCA, Fred Bennett. In 1986, Arthur Morris, the Trust's deputy chairman, wasn't reappointed and took retirement. The trustees appointed me to this position, a role I was to fulfil until Pat retired and I took over as the trust chairman.

The Bob Stand, at the northern extremity of the 'Hill', was demolished in the interests of progress and ground improvement. It was a bit of history lost, but happily the little stand that had witnessed a century of cricket and football was preserved, the building being relocated brick by brick to the North Sydney Oval just across the harbour. Pat Hills did a wonderful job of heading the reconstruction work of the whole SCG area, and it was a unanimous Trust decision to name the new stand after him. It was a sad moment, then, when the Greiner government removed his name and renamed it the O'Reilly Stand, after the great Australian spin bowler. We thought this was rather petty, given everything that Pat had achieved, but he acted with great dignity over the whole affair.

In 1981 there had been much talk about the South Melbourne Football Club relocating to Sydney. Fellow trustee Peter McMahon and I were asked by the trustees to negotiate with Alan Aylett, head of the Victorian Football League (VFL) in Melbourne. I agreed with the idea and thought it would be a good use for the ground, as well as an added fixture for our members. The VFL, too, were keen to come north, because they wanted to expand their game. Naturally, the move was unpopular among Melburnians, particularly South Melbourne fans, but what eventuated was to prove a landmark move for the SCG, with the Sydney Swans, in their eye-catching white and red outfits, providing Sydney with a brand-new sporting attraction. Hugely popular with the fans was the mighty Tony Lockett and, of course, the flamboyant Warwick Capper.

In the early years the Swans weren't financially successful; the SCG Trust helped to keep them afloat. In 1981 they played two games in Sydney, and then played a full season in 1982. In no time, they were a prized and permanent fixture at the SCG.

In 1985 the Trust became concerned about the heavy use of the SCG and decided that another ground was needed so as to protect the turf. With both cricket and football codes extending their seasons at the SCG, the traffic had reached saturation point. An arrangement was made with the Commonwealth government, which owned land, at the time occupied by the Army, at the rear of the Sports Ground. The area was cleared and the Sydney Football Stadium (SFS) plan was approved. Long discussions about the size and style of the new stadium took place, and a competition was won by Philip Cox Architects and the builders, Lend Lease, who had submitted a joint proposal. The capacity of the ground was debated at great length. Should it be 50 000, or smaller? Some thought 80 000 was the optimal capacity. Trends around the world indicated that stadiums were being built smaller due to reduced attendances brought about by television coverage of matches, so it was decided to restrict the capacity to 43 000. In hindsight, I would like to have settled on a capacity of 50 000. Since the stadium was built, some sports have expanded quite rapidly, making the SFS at times too small.

I found the SFS project highly exciting. The building committee comprised Pat Hills, Jim Bayutti, Noel Neate (the CEO) and myself. We had experience in this area. In 1985 we had rebuilt Parramatta Stadium and got it up and working. This stadium had been in trouble — it was dilapidated and wasn't being used. The government of the day asked the SCG Trust to take over the running of it. Our expertise in the redevelopment of the SCG meant that we were able to rebuild Parramatta Stadium and hand it over to the Trust debt free in 1988, when it was opened by Her Majesty Queen Elizabeth.

The Sydney Football Stadium, currently called Aussie Stadium, was duly built and finished on time without any government financial support, and proved an outstanding success. It was a new venture and an ambitious one. It had never been done before with private money. But we had done our homework. We knew it would work, being so close to the city; we would establish a sporting oasis with gymnasiums, a swimming pool and tennis courts. The idea was for it to become a health centre for members.

We set up a gold membership scheme to assist in financing the building. The design of the roof won an international architectural prize. It was an exciting time. Jim Bayutti was a brilliant engineer whose expertise was invaluable. The subcommittee met regularly with and checked on the builders and architects and reported back to the minister and the Trust.

Following the Greiner government's election victory that year, changes were made to the workings of the Trust, the main one being that the government in future would appoint both the chairman and his deputy, previously a task carried out by the trustees themselves. On the evening of Pat Hills' farewell dinner, I was just about to leave home for the function when I answered a call from a trustee, Doug Bain, who told me that the new minister for sport, Bob Rowland-Smith, was going to announce at the dinner that I would be the new chairman and Doug my deputy. The minister did just that, and the trustees all offered me their congratulations. I reflected for a moment that I hadn't been asked! It was certainly a great honour, and the eleven years during which I subsequently occupied that position were memorable.

The new government introduced a scheme in which trustees would be reimbursed for their out-of-pocket expenses incurred while carrying out their duties, but I didn't accept this. I felt it was a great enough honour just to be in the position. I paid my membership fees like every other SCG member, even though at times I was spending more than thirty hours a week on Trust business. I should add that having Noel Neate as my chief executive was a bonus; I rate him very highly as an operator.

Problems facing the Trust arose constantly during my chairmanship, none more difficult than when the Olympic Games were won for Sydney. The SCG and the SFS had enjoyed a wonderful run for their members, with relatively little competition from other sporting venues in Sydney. Our duty was to protect and look after our 20 000 members, including 8000 gold members.

A number of meetings with the Olympic Organising Committee gave us little support or encouragement, and they refused to allow us to meet with the body that controlled the Olympic Stadium. (In my view we should have been complementing each other, not competing against each other.) I am sure the hidden agenda was that the SCG Trust would fold, but they were underestimating our ability to maintain our position in the marketplace.

We played it fair and square, and supported the Olympic Games. We didn't want to jeopardise any of the events by going public on some of these issues. Several heated meetings took place with the minister, Michael Knight, and members of his department, but eventually some compromises were reached. To look after our members, if a sport was played at the Olympic Stadium that otherwise would have been held at the SFS, we would get up to 5000 tickets for our members. Rodney Cavalier, Alan Jones, John Cloney and John McCarthy provided strong support for me in the fight to protect the interests of our members.

The Olympic Stadium floated a company and then appointed a board, but the government needed our expertise to run the stadium. Between the two boards was the government, but it wouldn't allow us to talk to each other. Despite the fact that we were competing, there was still a lack of trust. There was concern that we at the SCG would take over. In truth, I feel that in the long term the SCG Trust will run the stadium at Homebush. The only way it will work is to have both stadiums under the one umbrella — one set of staff, the efficient allocation of events, and the sharing of the cash flow.

Stadium Australia, a private organisation, was being subsidised in many ways by the state government. On the other hand, the SCG Trust, a state government instrumentality, was receiving nothing and being penalised for it. The Olympics came and went, and what a wonderful Games it was, running like clockwork. The Olympic aquatic centre came under our control and, with the additional temporary seating, provided a marvellous spectacle. Many great events took place there and world records were broken.

The Sydney Swans continued to use the SCG, which had office accommodation on site, but it hadn't been an easy relationship. They seemed to have forgotten the early days when the Trust had assisted them financially. The Swans are a progressive organisation and have experienced many administrative changes, however, and our relationship has since improved greatly. Decisions regarding the Australian Football League (AFL) are made in Melbourne, and I'm sure that the officials there don't understand the Sydney scene. It has been suggested, for example, that the Swans play some matches at Stadium Australia. But with a big majority of their fans coming from the eastern suburbs of Sydney — a long distance from that venue — and with seating being a long distance from the action, I can't see the venture being a long-term success. The SCG venue, on the other hand, having cricket already on site, a magnificent practice centre, and the rugby Super Twelve home games so successful at the SFS, is very vibrant and very much the sporting centre of Sydney.

During my chairmanship, we always managed to finish the year in a financial position that was beneficial to our members, thus reducing our debts. Concerts were and still are a wonderful money-spinner. They enabled us to develop and fund the area to the benefit of sport, while also catering to the changing interests of the SCG's members.

When the NSW Tennis Association was moving out of White City, near Rushcutters Bay, we had a long, hard look at taking it over and establishing a tennis centre and country club. I think it could have worked, but negotiations became too complex and we walked away from it. The Trust had always looked for ways to make improvements for our members. On one occasion, when I was in London, I rang the Marylebone Cricket Club (MCC) secretary at Lords, to make an appointment. I couldn't get past his assistant secretary, who asked me what I wanted to see the secretary about. I mentioned that we would like to have an arrangement whereby our members could use their facilities when in London, as we have always extended that courtesy to MCC members visiting Sydney. The assistant secretary said that under no circumstances would this be possible, as they had a pre-existing arrangement with the Melbourne Cricket Ground. I then told him to inform his members that as from that moment I had withdrawn all privileges at the SCG for MCC members. He said that the secretary would be in Sydney for the forthcoming Test series. I replied that I hoped he had a ticket, otherwise he wouldn't be able to get into the ground.

The Surrey Cricket Club at London's The Oval, on the other hand, welcomed me and we put an arrangement in place, signed by the great English cricketers Ramon Subba Row and the Bedser twins, Alec and Eric, that has worked quite satisfactorily. Several years later, we were able to come to a similar arrangement with the MCC.

In the mid-1990s, a 'super' Rugby League competition was being proposed. A big disappointment for me occurred after Noel Neate had suggested that we should form a central Sydney Rugby League Club, based at the Sydney Football Stadium. The idea was to combine the inner-city clubs of Balmain, South Sydney and Eastern Suburbs, which would have established a truly powerful outfit. Several meetings took place with the three club presidents: Nick Politis of Eastern Suburbs, George Piggins of Souths and Neil Whittaker of Balmain. Things were going well until Eastern Suburbs, through Nick Politis, insisted that Easts should have 51 per cent control of the entity. This wouldn't have worked, and the idea collapsed. This was a pity because, in retrospect, it would have saved the League millions of dollars in court actions over the Super League wrangle. And what a great side it would have been! Soon afterwards, Balmain was forced to amalgamate with Western Suburbs, and South Sydney was expelled from the competition (though it has since been reinstated).

I retired as chairman of the SCG Trust in 2001, when Marie was appointed as the New South Wales governor. I resigned my position because I wanted to avoid any potentially awkward situations arising for Marie, who was in a position, as governor, to dismiss government trusts. I was honoured to have a stand at the SFS named after me and to be elected a life member of the Trust. I was also honoured to receive the following letter from Premier Bob Carr upon my retirement.

Dear Sir Nicholas,

I'm sorry that urgent Parliamentary business will prevent me from attending your farewell dinner as Chairman of the SCG Trust tonight.

I want to record — both personally and on behalf of the Government and people of New South Wales — my deep gratitude for the valuable work you've done at the Trust.

The SCG is one of those iconic Sydney places and to be Chairman of its Trust is a great privilege. Bill McKell counted it an honour second only to being NSW Premier and Labor Leader.

At this point after an immensely successful career in sport, business and public service you might reasonably have expected some peace and quiet. It was not to be.

As 'First Husband' of New South Wales you have important new duties in support of Her Excellency, your wife. Perhaps you picked up some tips from her when she was First Lady of Sydney during your mayoralty. I'm sure you will do it with great aplomb.

So you leave the SCG Trust stronger than ever, in a condition worthy of its fine traditions. For that you are owed a debt of gratitude.

Bob Carr
Premier of New South Wales

My days with the SCG Trust had afforded me the opportunity to meet many celebrities, visiting sportspeople, and entertainers such as Elton John, Denis Waterman and our own Simone Young, who informed me that she had once sold pies at the SCG. However, meeting Sir Donald Bradman on a number of occasions was the highlight. Marie and I also visited the Don at his Adelaide home, where I presented him with life membership of the SCG. He loved the SCG like no other ground. As a selector, he would examine the wicket square and recall how, in his halcyon days, he could see his own image reflected off the shiny Bulli soil surface, the famous soil for wickets brought in from Bulli, just south of Sydney.

The SCG reciprocated the Don's affection, for he was its favourite son. He had first visited the SCG as a twelve-year-old boy in the company of his father to see the first two days of the Ashes Test of the 1920–21 series. Many years later he wrote: 'My first glimpse of the ground, so immaculately groomed, really burnt its way into my memory. I hope the members of today will appreciate and cherish the venue they have inherited as I have done for over seventy years.' The Don made his highest score there — 452 not out against Queensland. The records show that attendances rose by 91 per cent when Bradman batted. He was admitted as a member in 1930.

Following Bradman's death in 2001, a memorial service was held on the SCG playing field. I pushed hard in my final years for a Walk of Honour inside the ground, which was eventually approved and constructed. Some thirty-three sporting champions who had performed on the SCG were chosen, with their names placed in a

The late Sir Donald Bradman had a long and affectionate love for the Sydney Cricket Ground, ranking it alongside Lords as his favourite. Marie and I visited the Don at his Adelaide home to present him with his life membership of the Sydney Cricket Ground. It was a thrilling occasion once again for us both to meet Australia's greatest sporting legend.

hat to determine the order of their plaques (inscribed with their sporting records and achievements) along the walkway. It seemed almost destiny that the name of Sir Donald Bradman was the first out of the hat. I left the Trust in wonderful shape and in good hands.

The premier of New South Wales, the Honourable Bob Carr, MP, officially opened the Walk of Honour on 4 January 2001. Selection was awarded to sportspeople for outstanding achievement as determined by the SCG and the Sports Ground Trust. Nominees must have achieved success in their chosen sport at the highest

Unveiling the Sydney Cricket Ground's Walk of Honour. My grandchildren, Nicholas, Persephone and Victoria, and son-in-law Malcolm Moir, are alongside me for the Walk's opening. Plaques were placed along the walkway recognising thirty-three sporting champions, and inscribed with their sporting records and achievements.

level of available competition and competed in sports traditionally and/or formerly played at the Sydney Cricket Ground, Sydney Sports Ground or Sydney Football Stadium. These achievements could be by way of contribution to sporting history, heritage or culture.

Here is the list of Walk of Honour inductees (in alphabetical order):

Trevor Allan OAM, *Rugby*

Arthur Beetson OAM, *Rugby League*

Richie Benaud OBE, *Cricket*

Sir Donald Bradman AC, *Cricket*

Bill Brown OAM, *Cricket*

Ken Catchpole, *Rugby*

Clive Churchill AM, *Rugby League*

Hon Michael Cleary AO, *Rugby, Rugby League, Athletics*

Betty Cuthbert AM MBE, *Athletics*

Alan Davidson AM MBE, *Cricket*

Mark, Glen and Gary Ella, *Rugby*

Reg Gasnier AM, *Rugby League*

The Gregorys (Dave, Ned, Sid and Jack), *Cricket*

Neil Harvey MBE, *Cricket*

Keith Holman MBE, *Rugby League*

Marjorie Jackson-Nelson, AC *Athletics*

Joe Marston MBE, *Soccer*

Marlene Mathews AO, *Athletics*

Dally Messenger, *Rugby League*

Keith Miller MBE, *Cricket*

Arthur Morris MBE, *Cricket*

Decima Norman MBE, *Athletics*

Norman O'Neill, *Cricket*

John Raper MBE, *Rugby League*

St George Dragons, *Rugby League*

Sir Nicholas Shehadie AC OBE, *Rugby*

Bob Simpson AM, *Cricket*

John, Ken and Dick Thornett, *Rugby, Rugby League*

Cyril Towers, *Rugby*

Victor Trumper, *Cricket*

Doug Walters MBE, *Cricket*

John Warren MBE, *Soccer*

Colin Windon, *Rugby*

12 RUGBY REVISITED, 1979-87

One Friday in 1979 I received a call from Peter Falk, a good friend and member of the executive committee of the New South Wales Rugby Union (NSWRU). Peter begged me to stand for chairman of the Union. I asked when the election was to be held, and he replied that it was that very evening. 'No way,' I said. He explained that there were some personality clashes that could be detrimental to the game and that I was the only person who could defuse the situation. He rang back after a short while, asking for an urgent answer.

After giving the matter some serious (if brief) thought, I decided I would do it. I had been a director for the past five years of the

Sydney Turf Club (STC), a position I enjoyed very much, and giving it up wasn't a decision to make hastily. I decided I would have to give up that position. It would have been too much work to attempt to do both jobs, and I wouldn't be able to do justice to either. I felt I had a bigger obligation to rugby.

Sir Clyde Kennedy, the chairman of the Sydney Turf Club had been manager of the first New South Wales rugby team I was in that toured Queensland. I had always had a great love for thoroughbred racing, especially since I came from the Randwick district with all its stables and the racecourse close by. I had been on the fringes of the sport, racing a few horses with friends, including former sportsmen Alan Davidson and Don Furness and businessmen Sir Eric Neal and John Utz.

My association with Tattersalls Club in Sydney brought me even closer to the racing community, for it was there I met people such as Tom Powell, George Mousally, Ken Ranger, Peter Twigg and Doug Jordan, who were all good friends and supporters of mine. This ensured my election to the board of the STC. Being a director of the club brought me into contact with people from all walks of life whom I wouldn't normally have come into contact with. As chairman of the membership committee, I had a lot to do with members and membership issues. I would walk around the concourses at the track to see how everything was going and what improvements needed to be made. I really enjoyed it.

I wanted to pay the STC the courtesy of telling them of my decision to give up my directorship prior to any announcement being made, but they wouldn't be meeting until the following

Monday morning. The NSWRU agreed that if I was appointed, they promised not to make an announcement until the following Monday afternoon.

I was duly appointed chairman, and so I resigned from the STC committee and the duties that I had thoroughly enjoyed. It was some years since I had been involved in any rugby committees, which meant that I had to quickly get up to speed. Something of a power game had developed, and while I was sure the various individuals on the board all had the game at heart, they were working in different directions. It was immediately pretty clear that there were problems.

It wasn't too long before everything had settled down, though. My position as chairman of the NSWRU gave me a seat on the Australian Rugby Union (ARU) board, where I was elected deputy president to Bill McLaughlin. In those days, there was no chairman of the ARU — the president was at the helm for all decisions made; today he is only the ceremonial chief, while the chairman looks after the day-to-day operations.

I could never understand the hostility that seemed to exist between the New South Wales and Queensland bodies. They were really parochial, yet both groups were dedicated to the game and, in their own way, contributed a great deal. One thing was clear: New South Wales was travelling in a different direction from the rest of rugby.

After a year as NSWRU chairman, in 1980 I was elected president of the ARU following Bill McLaughlin's retirement. Our offices were in Crane Place, on the same floor as the NSWRU, which wasn't an ideal situation. New South Wales was becoming much more entrepreneurial and was very involved with private enterprises and sponsorship. Their chief executive, Ken Elphick, and chairman, Ross Turnbull, and his committee were negotiating to get a ground for New South Wales, no doubt encouraged by Queensland's spectacular success with its new venue at Brisbane's Ballymore. With the Wran government sympathetic to their proposal, they took over from Concord Council what was to be known as Waratah Park, formerly Concord Oval. I resisted the idea that the ARU should get involved with this development. Having one's own ground was fine, but to spend millions of dollars on somebody else's ground on a lease arrangement didn't appeal to me. In my opinion, it just wasn't good business.

My feelings about the unsuitability of Concord Oval as a headquarters ground were supported by the players, notably David Campese, who had this to say in his book *A Wing and a Prayer*:

Thankfully, common sense had at last prevailed among the Australian Rugby Union and the authorities had bitten the bullet and turned away from Concord Oval, that unloved, unlovely ground out in the western suburbs of the city. How anyone conceived that place as the future home of Australian international rugby is beyond belief: always was beyond the belief of the players. We told the relevant people in authority as much at the time the whole crazy project was being considered, but, of course, those people never listen to players, what do they know? They only play the game. So millions of dollars were invested in Concord and millions of dollars were washed down the drains of that part of the city ... Concord was not only miles away from anywhere, it was not even in an area which had the character and appeal of Paddington, which is close to the old Sydney Cricket Ground where the rugby Tests used to be played. Paddington is filled with pubs and clubs, and whenever a major Test match is played in Sydney, you will find thousands of fans inside the pubs and restaurants, before and after the game, having a beer with their mates or a meal later that evening. It is a bit like Richmond and Twickenham. Richmond is the place to head for after a Twickenham international: it has some great pubs and eating houses and is nearby ... Concord is and was always going to be a graveyard for international rugby.

The talk of the money to be expended concerned me greatly. In order to protect any assets the ARU had, we moved out of Crane Place, where we were renting, and purchased the then vacant National Bank premises at Kingsford. We were only a few kilometres out of the city and in close proximity to the airport at Mascot, and the Sydney Cricket Ground. The move was most successful and met with the approval of our international and interstate delegates. And it turned out to be a great financial decision: when the ARU later moved to North Sydney, it made a hefty profit.

The 1981–82 Wallaby tour of the United Kingdom, for which I was tour manager, was to be the last of the marathon tours.

RUGBY FLASHBACK

It had been on my conscience for something like thirty-four years and at last I was able to make a formal apology. I was managing the 1981 Wallaby touring team in the United Kingdom, where one of the feature events was the function hosted by the British Sportsman's Club at the famous Savoy Hotel in London. As manager, I had to reply to the welcome from the club president, Ted Heath, former British prime minister and yachting enthusiast. I confessed that on my first Wallaby tour in 1947–48 I had 'borrowed' Lord Wavell Wakefield's bowler hat for a visit to Paris and had failed to return it. Lord Wakefield smiled and called out from the audience, 'You showed good taste, son.'

Three of the four international matches were lost, all by relatively narrow margins, but I had the great joy of seeing a bunch of brilliantly talented young players who, in the years ahead, would inspire a resurgence of Australian rugby. The Ella brothers — Mark, Glen and Gary — Michael Hawker, Simon Poidevin, Michael O'Connor, Brendan Moon, Andrew Slack, Steve Williams and Roger Gould … this was a preview showing of the great days that lay ahead.

The tour was dogged by appalling weather: cold, rain and snow. The Australian players, brought up on firm, fast playing surfaces, were shackled in ankle-deep mud. Even so, this tour team recorded sixteen wins and a draw in twenty-three matches played, with a 16–12 victory over Ireland and losses to Scotland (15–24), Wales (13–18) and England (11–15). Paul McLean, who had built a reputation for accurate goal-kicking, was off-key with the boot throughout the tour, mainly due to the condition of the grounds, and a number of games that should have been won were lost. However, we built a fine record for strong defensive play, reflected in the statistic of eight tries scored and only three conceded in the four international matches.

Injuries plagued the tour. After a training mishap, hooker Bruce Malouf returned home with a broken leg, without having played a match. John Hipwell, the half-back whom we felt would be the mainstay of the tour, missed many games through persistent injuries.

The final fixture against the Barbarians in Cardiff was cancelled due to heavy snowfalls and an unplayable ground, denying some farewell glory for Paul McLean, Mark Loane and John Hipwell. Overall, it was a disappointing tour statistically, but a positive note to come out of it was the great strides achieved in the building of outstanding Australian Wallaby sides in the years to follow.

The years that I was president of the Australian Rugby Union, from 1980 to 1987, saw many changes take place. One major change occurred in schoolboy rugby in 1986–87, when many players at this level were experiencing neck injuries, some of them major. I felt that something had to be done — and quickly. I had several meetings with Dr John Yeo, head of the spinal unit at Sydney's North Shore Hospital, who was also very keen on sport. The private schools of Sydney were contemplating withdrawing rugby as one of their school sports. As president of the ARU, I called a meeting with as many prop forwards as I could muster. Every Wallaby prop available attended. About thirty of us gathered in a room. (I had never seen so many cauliflower ears and bent noses in one gathering before!) The first question I asked was why players stood a metre apart from their opponents and packed down opposite them with a forceful bang when engaging a scrum. Some of the answers given were quite hilarious, but it was agreed that the players were only letting their opponents know that they meant business and endeavouring to establish their superiority. Everyone agreed that it was important to keep one's neck straight and feet balanced at all times. With the input from this meeting and the medical advice of John Yeo, we came up with a change to schoolboy rugby scrummaging. Our proposal was that when the front row was bound, they would engage with the opposition without the customary force, place their feet closer to the centre of the scrum (which makes the scrum higher) and keep their necks straight, which then keeps their backs straight.

I then called a meeting with all the schools' headmasters and explained to them our proposal, which I said was aimed at avoiding further neck injuries and making schoolboy rugby much safer. The proposal was adopted, and the new approach to scrums in schoolboy rugby has practically eliminated neck injuries. Dr Yeo was extremely happy with the result. We later heard that New Zealand and South Africa also adopted this method for schoolboy rugby.

In the mid-1980s I attended in Brisbane the funeral of the wife of Joe French, then president of the Queensland Rugby Union, who later became president of the ARU. On my return to Sydney the next morning I went out to my factory in Lewisham, where I was handed a message to call Steve Liebmann from Channel Nine's 'Today Show'. I was often interviewed on TV and radio about South African rugby, and expected that this was the reason for Steve's call. When I finally got through to Steve, whom I had known for many years, I said to him, 'I have nothing further to say about South Africa.'

He said, 'It's not South Africa I want to talk to you about.' He asked whether I had seen Bert Newton's 'Tonight Show' on TV the night before. I said I hadn't. He said that Newton had interviewed the British actor Richard Harris, live from New York, where he was playing King Arthur in the musical *Camelot*. Newton had asked Harris about his forthcoming visit to Australia. Evidently, at the end of the interview Newton had asked him what he particularly wished to see and do while in Australia. Harris had replied that he wanted to meet Nick Shehadie, whom he had seen play in county Cork, Ireland, against his favourite team, Munster, in 1947. (Apparently Bert Newton, who was based in Melbourne, had no idea who I was.)

Steve asked me if I would appear on the 'Today Show' and surprise Richard Harris. I agreed. On the appointed day, I arrived at the Channel Nine studios with an Australian rugby jersey to present to the actor. The problem was that the official jersey of the current day was gold, but back in 1947 we had played in green.

I was immediately ushered into a private room so that I wouldn't be seen. I could see and hear Harris being interviewed, and at last Steve mentioned that apparently Harris had wanted to meet Nick Shehadie. Harris explained that he had always wanted to be a rugby player and to play for Munster. He said that he liked the way I played and had followed my career as a rugby player. I then walked onto the set and surprised him, presenting him with the jersey, which he adored. (I told him a white lie and said it was mine.) It was a wonderful occasion for me, as I had loved seeing him in films. I particularly admired his beautiful speaking voice. He passed away recently. In an obituary, he was quoted as saying that he wanted to be buried in his beloved Munster jersey.

* * *

During my time as president of the ARU, there was a lot of pressure on players to tour while still being expected to remain amateurs. It was clear that something had to be done or we would lose our players. South Africa was banned and isolated, and there was talk of rebel tours of that country, all of which made things difficult. I had always felt that rugby was a game that could be marketed successfully around the world, and I was concerned that some non-rugby entrepreneur or organisation might step in and take over marketing of the sport and do the wrong thing by it. In cricket, Kerry Packer, with encouragement and support from the game's leading international players, had introduced World Series Cricket with its spectacular-coloured clothing and day/night matches that filled the stadiums. The traditional game of cricket was under siege. The established cricket authorities fought for a period of time, but theirs was a lost cause. Packer, fortunately, with the very future of the game at heart, offered the administrators a lifeline — the introduction of one-day cricket —

that ultimately they accepted, and since then the game hasn't looked back.

So, if it seemed inevitable that rugby would go the same way, why not do it ourselves? In any case, the pressure we were placing on our players, and the commitment we required of them, was ridiculous. This led me to look long and hard at establishing a world tournament, to be held every four years, to preserve our beloved game of rugby. This would also cut down on long tours, which were a hardship for the players. Rugby was the only sport that didn't have a world competition event. It was time.

13 THE WORLD CUP

And the winner is ... Rugby's World Cup! Inaugurated in 1987 after a troubled and hazardous start, the World Cup has transformed the code into a worldwide sporting spectacle, exceeded only by the Olympic Games and World Cup Soccer. In the process, the game has plunged headlong into professionalism, where leading players rank among the world's most lavishly paid sportsmen.

The 1999 World Cup, held in Wales, was a triumphant success, earning a mountainous £70 million (approximately A$200 million) in revenue and attracting an estimated 3.5 billion television viewers across the globe. Yet, the initial formation days saw many doubters.

The Home Unions — England, Ireland, Scotland and Wales, where the game was securely entrenched through an almost ancient tradition — set up a dour opposition to the proposed revolutionary changes. But the battle was won with the compelling drive coming from Down Under. A New Zealand rugby official labelled it 'The Nick and Dick Show'. (Dick Littlejohn was my counterpart in New Zealand rugby.)

The concept of a Rugby World Cup wasn't new to the Australian Rugby Union. In the late 1950s, two Manly Club stalwarts, Harold Tolhurst and Jock Kellaher, both international identities, proposed such an event and were duly shunned by the administrators, who considered the idea not to be in the game's best interests. Any changes to the international rules and regulations would have to be sanctioned by the international board, which then comprised France, Australia, New Zealand and South Africa, plus the dominating Home Unions.

In my day, rugby was strictly an amateur game, and there was fierce resistance to any hint of professionalism. A player who wrote a book about his experiences would have been disqualified from playing, as would any player who was paid expenses prior to a tour.

The ARU thought that by introducing a World Cup we could have a big celebration once every four years and reduce the number of tours the rest of the time. The money earned would flow to the various countries involved to support and promote the game locally. And the players would generally have a lot more fun.

Prior to my return to rugby, the ARU was approached by a group of Sydney businessmen who said they were interested in providing financial support to a World Cup if the Union would submit a proposal. The ARU president of the day, Bill McLaughlin, failed to arouse any enthusiasm from his board — most likely because of the domination of the Home Unions and the fact that their objections were well known. At the time, I was very much involved in horse racing through the Sydney Turf Club, as well as in other business interests, and wasn't aware of the burgeoning World Cup movement. When I returned to rugby as chairman of the NSWRU in 1979, I automatically had a seat on the ARU executive, as mentioned before. It was only when I was elected president in 1980 that I became involved in the World Cup proceedings. The job was difficult — we weren't paid, and we were criticised more often than not.

There was a whirlwind of events, all taking place at the same time — mainly in the Northern Hemisphere. In 1982, a London-based promoter, Neil Durden-Smith, representing International Sport Marketing (ISM), visited Sydney and met with John Howard (ARU treasurer), John Dedrick (secretary) and myself to outline ISM's plans for a World Cup promotion. Momentum was building behind the scenes. They asked if we would raise the matter at the International Rugby Football Board (IRFB) meeting in March 1983. (They needed a country to raise the matter on their behalf.) I agreed to raise with my union the idea of having our delegates bring the proposal to the IRFB.

At the next board meeting, Durden-Smith and Gideon Lloyd, both of whom were well known in international rugby circles, discussed the proposal with ARU delegates on the IRFB. They revealed that if the IRFB approved the scheme and the tournament went ahead, the top eight unions who constituted the board would receive £587 500 each, and the other four invited unions £75 000 each. Similar approaches had been made to other international board delegates to get someone to propose to the board the idea of a World Cup. These meetings were the first occasion on which the proposal had been made directly to me, and I raised it with the ARU board. 'What have we got to lose?' I said. I could see the benefits for rugby, because it was the only major sport that didn't have a big international event. I could see that it would be easily marketable. The ARU board gave me their full support, but the proposal was given a mixed reception by the international board and went no further. I have never been a member of the IRFB.

Meanwhile, following the 1981–82 Australian tour to the United Kingdom, we learned that David Lord, a Sydney-based sports journalist who had led a tour group of rugby fans on the tour, had endeavoured to set up a World Rugby circus using international sports promoters. Although he failed to get his idea off the ground at the time, he succeeded in getting commitments from many of the top Australian players. Not many people took him seriously or thought he had had a chance of getting even that far.

I knew I had to act quickly after I had a meeting with a number of the senior Wallaby players, with whom I had a very close relationship. They admitted that they had agreed to sign with Lord. The situation had become serious. Their actions were a breach of the rules of amateurism, and they could have been disqualified from playing rugby, but I assured them that our meeting would be confidential and that they wouldn't be penalised because they had been honest and up-front, and this had given me the platform to take the initiative.

The game was at a crossroads; something had to be done — and done quickly. There was a clear movement towards professionalism. New Zealand was also having problems: there were plans afoot for a rebel tour of South Africa for which the players would be paid.

I called an unofficial meeting of my executive — John Howard, Norbet Byrne, Ross Turnbull and John Dedrick — and stressed to them that if we were to save our game and not lose it to some entrepreneur, we would have to act promptly and organise a World Cup. Also, rugby people must be involved. All were in agreement. My initial idea was to invite England to play Australia to celebrate our bicentenary in 1988. The international board designated the tours years ahead — which countries were to play in various competitions — so we would need to apply without delay to hold the 1988 game against England. This idea soon transformed into a bigger ambition: to hold a World Cup in 1988 instead.

Our recommendation, put to the ARU council in 1983, that we place before the International Rugby Board at its annual meeting (to be held the following March) our proposal to host a World Cup in 1988, the year that we were to celebrate Australia's 200th birthday, was carried unanimously. However, when we later learned that New Zealand had lodged a similar request to host a World Cup in 1987, it was decided that I should visit Cec Blazey, my counterpart in New Zealand, and discuss joining forces. Cec and I had built up a very close relationship over the years and he was a most respected figure on the international scene — he had much more influence than I did. He was on the international board, where he wielded considerable power. We decided to recommend to our unions that we join forces for the 1987 date, locking in a World Cup every four years and avoiding a clash with the scheduled years of the Olympic Games, the Commonwealth Games and World Cup Soccer. This would give us a permanent rugby-only year. We proceeded to lodge a joint proposal. It felt like a natural progression, given the increasing pressure for professionalism within the game and the marketers beating down our doors.

When it came to the vital vote in 1984, we would have the assurance of four votes out of sixteen. The IRFB reluctantly agreed to both Australia and New Zealand submitting a detailed feasibility study and business plan before the board's 1985 annual meeting. They never really thought we would have the report completed on time. Australia and New Zealand formed a joint committee to see the proposal through and to formulate the study. Dick Littlejohn, with whom I had had difficulties in the past, chaired the New Zealand contingent comprising Ivan Vodanovich, Tom Johnson (later replaced by Russ Thomas) and Barry Usmar, the New Zealand secretary. I led our group of Norbert Byrne, John Howard and John Dedrick. The committee met regularly — on meeting Dick again we soon resolved our differences and became firm friends. After several months of hard work, we finalised our submission and forwarded it on within the prescribed time.

I had always felt that the IRFB was too far removed from the players and didn't fully understand their needs. I was never interested in becoming an IRFB delegate myself, although I had many friends who were members, including John Kendall-Carpenter, whom I had first met in Penzance, in Cornwall, in 1947 at the outset of the 1947–48 Wallaby Tour; Ron Dawson, whom I had propped alongside in the 1958 Barbarians game against Australia; and Keith Rowlands, who had played for Wales (and whom I had played against). It was decided by our joint committee that Dick and I should endeavour to meet with all the UK unions and present our case, in the hope that they would instruct their representatives how to vote when the time came.

South Africa, as a member of the IRFB, had two votes but couldn't participate in the proposed World Cup because both the Australian and New Zealand governments wouldn't allow the team entry visas, due to political sanctions. South Africa was a great rugby nation, but it was isolated because of its government's stand on apartheid. Until he learned the truth, Danie Craven, the South African Rugby president, blamed me for Australia's stand against South Africa. He had been told many lies by jealous and ambitious Australian officials. It was some years before he apologised and told me the full story.

Dr Roger Vanderfield, who was to become chairman of the IRFB when the vital vote was taken, performed a mammoth role at his own expense and, without anyone knowing, made a private visit to South Africa. Roger is most respected throughout the rugby world and was close to many of the South African officials, especially Dr Craven. He visited several of the unions in the republic and was invited to address the annual meeting of the South African Rugby board in Cape Town, where he received a warm welcome. He had refereed the Springboks on two tours of Australia, including the incredibly difficult visit of 1971. The 'Boks also appreciated the respect Roger had shown them by making his visit, and this was later to play a big part in their final decision.

Dick Littlejohn and I received a mixed reception from the UK media, which didn't seem to realise how determined we were. They didn't take us particularly seriously — they thought it was all pie-in-the-sky stuff. We travelled to Cardiff to meet the executive of the Welsh Rugby Union. The meeting was held in the palatial president's room at Cardiff Arms Park. I spoke for about forty minutes on why they should support our proposal if they wished to support the game. If they didn't, I warned, any entrepreneur could take our game and market it around the world. If we took the opportunity to do it ourselves, we could ensure that the game would be controlled by rugby people. They had to realise that the game was much bigger than just in the UK, I said, and that many countries needed international exposure and experience. After answering their barrage of questions, I asked for an expression of interest. There was complete silence in the room; things didn't seem to be going too well. After many minutes, the late Ken Harris, the long-serving treasurer of the Welsh Rugby Union, stood up, paused, and said, 'I support the proposal one hundred per cent.' There were no dissenters. We were now on our way.

We then proceeded to Dublin to meet the Irish. Having spoken with their officials a year earlier, I wasn't anticipating any support. We arrived at the airport in Dublin at 2 a.m. in the middle of a wild snowstorm. There were no taxis available to take us to our hotel, but we managed to get a lift with a group of rugby enthusiasts, all of us crammed like sardines into a very small car with our luggage tied to the roof. We were to confer with the Irish officials the next morning, prior to the Ireland–England International match.

The next day, the snow was so heavy the match was called off and our meeting was cancelled because the delegates couldn't get to the city. It was agreed that we would meet in Edinburgh before the Scottish International the following week. In the meantime, I visited BBC Enterprises at Shepherd's Bush on the advice of Cliff Morgan, the former great Welsh and Lions fly-half and BBC broadcaster. I offered them the television and marketing rights for the proposed 1987 World Cup for US$6 million. They gave me short shrift, telling me that it simply wouldn't get off the ground, as the IRFB wouldn't agree to such an event. I felt a bit deflated after that meeting.

In Scotland, we had dinner with the Scottish executives and their wives on the evening prior to our meeting with their full board. I was ridiculed by their treasurer, Gordon Masson, who told me in no uncertain terms that rugby was *their* game and they didn't need us; a World Cup would be staged over his dead body, he said. I didn't back off. 'When the World Cup is held,' I said, 'don't bother coming.' The irony was that in 1991, when the World Cup took place in the UK, Masson was the president of Scotland Rugby Union and escorted Princess Anne onto the field several times. When he saw me, I confronted him and pinched him to see if he was still alive!

Not surprisingly, the Scottish board was dead against any change. When we met with Ireland later that morning, they too opposed any concept of a World Cup. What both these unions failed to realise was that they were at odds with their own players, who supported the proposal. The French Rugby president, Albert Ferrasse, was a real dictator when it came to rugby matters, and I admired him very much. We knew we had Albert's support, even though he didn't attend our meeting with the French Rugby Union, and we went through the motions. I was referred to by the French as 'Petit Albert' — quite a compliment. We didn't know how England would move. Dick and I both addressed some thirty of their delegates and we thought we had a chance. With so many people present, it was a difficult meeting.

Our big day came when we were to meet with the IRFB. Dick and I had discussed our strategy and resolved that, having come this far, we wouldn't take a backward step. The meeting took place on the top floor of the East India Club in St James Square in the centre of London, in a large and well-worn room. Pleasantries were exchanged and then the tough talk began. I seemed to be the target for questioning, and there weren't too many friendly faces among the UK delegates. The Southern Hemisphere was accused of making the game professional. I replied, 'It's you delegates who are doing that, by scheduling so many long tours which place too many demands on the players.' The World Cup, we argued, would reduce the number of tours by celebrating the game every four years with a great tournament.

Australia was accused by the Welsh delegate, Hermes Evans, of paying our players' expenses up-front, contrary to the amateur rules of the IRFB. He singled out Peter Falk, the Australian team manager at the Hong Kong Rugby Sevens the year before. He had me over a barrel until Bob Weighill, the honorary secretary of the IRFB whom I had played against in 1947, nudged me under the table and passed me a note saying that England had done the same thing on their recent tour to the United States. I then countered Evans by saying that because England had done the same on its tour of the US, we thought it was the correct procedure. That stopped them in their tracks. *Thank the Lord for old friends*, I thought. I was also asked whether, if the IRFB refused our proposal, we would go it alone. I said I would answer that question after they made their decision. (New Zealand and Australia had, in fact, agreed to go it alone, if necessary, an action that would have blown the rugby world apart.)

I had mixed feelings when we walked away from the meeting. The final vote would be taken at the board's meeting in Paris, in March 1985. We had done all we could, and now it was up to the delegates. Roger Vanderfield and Ross Turnbull, our two delegates, had done everything in their power, and we knew that Australia, New Zealand and France were okay.

When the votes were finally taken, the English and Welsh votes were split, with Kendall-Carpenter of England and Keith Rowlands of Wales siding with us. South Africa chose not to vote, and both Ireland and Scotland voted against the proposal. Each country had two votes, so the final tally was: Australia two for; New Zealand two for; France two for; Wales one for, one against; England one for, one against; Scotland two against; and Ireland two against. We had won — eight to six! It was a great victory for rugby.

Now the hard work began, with the IRFB stubbornly rejecting the title of World Cup, and substituting the William Webb Ellis Tournament as the name. Ultimately, though, the name 'World Cup' stuck. They appointed a subcommittee to oversee the operation, headed by John Kendall-Carpenter (England), Keith Rowlands (Wales), Ron Dawson (Ireland), Ross Turnbull (Australia) and Bob Stuart (New Zealand). I think this committee met in just about every part of the world.

Sponsorship wasn't easy to come by. I encouraged the organising committee to allow me to engage Wilf Barker, an experienced entrepreneur in sports marketing who was well known internationally, to represent World Cup Pty Limited, the name we gave the company, in all its marketing negotiations. (We had to form a company to sign agreements.) I came to an arrangement with Wilf, saying that I would give him $50 000 — no more — and that he had to do it for that amount, for the game. After I twisted his arm, he said he would do it. He had a big reputation in the television and sponsorship fields and had been experiencing knock-backs in a lot of places. In the UK I was virtually ridiculed in the press — they said it would never work. But I was determined to keep going. We advertised around the world for someone to purchase the marketing arm. We had no idea what it was worth, but I had a lot of help from Wilf. There were several tenders and we eventually appointed Westnally, an English organisation that formed a branch company in New Zealand. After an all-night meeting with our lawyer, Michael Gray, at the

JOINT CHAIRMEN
1987 INAUGURAL RUGBY WORLD CUP COMMITTEE

Sir Nicholas Shehadie
O.B.E.
Australian Rugby Union

John MacGregor
Kendall-Carpenter
C.B.E., M.A., A.C.P.
International Rugby Board

R.J. (Dick) Littlejohn
Q.S.M.
New Zealand
Rugby Union

The battle to introduce Rugby's World Cup was fierce and desperate. Here are the three joint chairmen who formed the 1987 inaugural Rugby World Cup committee, which made it all possible.

Travelodge Hotel in Rushcutters Bay, in Sydney, we finally signed the successful tenderer at 6 a.m. We were running out of time and had to act quickly. They bought the rights for US$5 million. I asked for US$1 million on signing the contract and we locked in that money. Interest rates were high back then, and the interest we earned paid for all travel expenses. We needed all the money we could get. When the international board appointed a subcommittee of seven, we had to cover their expenses as well: they attended meetings in various locations around the world, including Thailand, Auckland, Hong Kong, the United States and Sydney. By the time of the first kick-off of the World Cup, the expenses were all paid for.

RUGBY FLASHBACK

Everything seemed in place for the staging of the 1987 inaugural World Cup. Well, almost. We didn't have a trophy! The England delegate, John Kendall-Carpenter, sent out the alarm and we urged him to urgently find a suitable trophy in the United Kingdom. He went to Garrards (the Crown jewellers) and found a copy of an original piece made by Carrington & Co. of London in 1906, designed by the Huguenot silversmith Paul de Lemerie. It was made of silver gilt, and we completed the purchase for £6000. The Home Unions had strenuously but unsuccessfully tried to call the event the William Webb Ellis trophy, recalling the famous schoolboy at Rugby who first ran with the ball. But he isn't forgotten. The Cup is now known far and wide as 'Bill'.

World Cup Pty Limited had John Kendall-Carpenter, Dick Littlejohn and myself as directors. The company, which was registered in Australia, became the vehicle for all commercial contracts. The combined organising committee agreed on sixteen countries participating in the inaugural World Cup, with the final to be held in Auckland: Australia, New Zealand, France, England, Ireland, Wales, Scotland, Argentina, Fiji, Japan, Italy, the United States, Zimbabwe, Canada, Tonga and Romania. It was crucial to include Japan because of the advertising dollar. Shiggy Konno, an old and dear friend, was head of Japan Rugby, and I knew that once England was involved, Japan would follow. I flew to Tokyo, met with Shiggy, and he was right behind us.

A few hiccups occurred, none worse than the military coup in Fiji that occurred in May 1987. There was a cloud over whether the Fijians would be able to participate.

Venues and hotel accommodations were put in place, and it was decided that Eden Park, Auckland, would be the best venue to hold the final. New Zealand and Australia shared all the up-front costs, which would be reimbursed. Any profits would then be shared among the participating countries. We registered the logo, with the sixteen bars on the football representing the sixteen competing countries. This logo is still being used today.

The IRFB, which oversaw the World Cup, at times proved very difficult, and it was inevitable that a confrontation would take place. John Kendall-Carpenter rang to forewarn me that there was a move to have his committee of five appointed directors on the board of World Cup Pty Limited, which would have meant

New Zealand and Australia losing control. I informed Dick and we then contacted our respective executive committees, seeking their permission to stand fast. We were summoned to a meeting with the committee in Los Angeles at the Beverly Wiltshire Hotel, where we were asked to remain outside while they discussed certain matters. It was schoolboy stuff. They had no idea that we knew what they were debating, but when we were admitted, some people had their heads lowered. When the subject was raised, I emphatically rejected the whole proposal, stating that my union supported me one hundred per cent. I informed them that they needed a two-thirds majority by the existing board. Dick's union also gave him the authority to stand fast, so he didn't mince words either. They were flabbergasted. We then walked out. The matter was never raised again.

South Africa said that they fully understood that we couldn't invite them, but decided not to vote. We are indeed indebted to Roger Vanderfield for his early discussions with the South African rugby authorities, which convinced them not to vote against the World Cup. Deciding instead not to vote at all, they acted with dignity in the interests of rugby. An invitation would be issued to them and they would graciously decline. We had Western Samoa standing by in case of any country defaulting, especially as we hadn't heard from Fiji. K.D.D., a Japanese communications company, became the major sponsor, providing US$3.25 million. We invited all the team managers to visit Australia and New Zealand to familiarise themselves with the venues and accommodations.

We had over 1000 volunteers in Australia and New Zealand. To our delight, the Fijians arrived at the appointed time. Dinners were held in both Auckland and Brisbane prior to the Cup commencing.

The first game, held on 22 May 1987, was New Zealand versus Italy in Auckland. After the kick-off, Dick looked across at me. We shared a huge smile and agreed that we had made it, against all the odds. 'The Nick and Dick Show' proved a tremendous success, producing a profit of over US$2.5 million. The World Cup continues to go from strength to strength — it is now the third most watched sporting event in the world. I retired, finally, from rugby after the World Cup and was made a life member of the ARU. The game had now changed forever, but within our terms. My aim throughout had been to preserve the game of rugby that had been so good to me.

14 SPECIAL BROADCASTING SERVICE, 1981–99

My appointment as chairman of the Special Broadcasting Service (SBS) proved to be one of the most stimulating challenges I have ever undertaken. In June 1981, I was chairing a meeting as president of the Australian Rugby Union in Rugby House, Crane Place, Sydney, when I was handed a note from the switchboard operator asking me to call Bob Lansdowne, secretary of the Department of Communications, as soon as possible. I had had many dealings with Bob when I was lord mayor of Sydney, working on the Woolloomooloo redevelopment scheme, when he headed the Department of Urban and Regional Development (known as DURD) under the minister Tom Uren. I called Bob back after my meeting, and he said that the minister for communications, Ian Sinclair, wanted to appoint me chairman of the Special Broadcasting Service. I think Bob must have put my name forward for the job.

SBS was in its infancy and I knew very little about it. I was to call the minister the next day with my answer, which gave me the opportunity to consult Marie, whose advice is always sound and practical. She was in hospital at the time, recovering from major neck surgery. When I told her about the offer of appointment, she urged me to accept it. She reasoned that SBS could be a great and unique operation for Australia, but that there was always the danger that someone with extreme political views might be put in charge, which would be detrimental to the country. I have always regarded my approach to most things as being non-political, and I could see Marie's point.

SBS Television had just gone to air, although SBS Radio had been operating in a very amateurish manner for several years. Television was small-time then, because only certain parts of Sydney and Melbourne could receive the signal, mainly due to its UHF frequency. All the other broadcasters were on the VHF band. Prior to my appointment I had never given the organisation much thought; I was busy doing other things. Besides, you couldn't receive very clear reception, and it was only on air for a few hours a day.

I had little or no experience with the media — in particular, the electronic media. However, after much discussion and on Marie's advice, I agreed to take up the challenge. I rang the minister,

Ian Sinclair, and accepted the appointment. (I had met Ian in my early rugby days.) After that discussion, I had a briefing from Bob Lansdowne. The idea was to stabilise SBS, as there were many problems, due mainly to the fact that it was still an 'experiment'. SBS was only established because the ABC wasn't meeting its charter, which stated that it should accommodate people of non-English-speaking backgrounds. I would be answerable directly to the minister.

For many years, SBS had been at the crossroads — one of its continuing problems was the question of whether or not the funding would continue. I decided to go in with a positive outlook. It did not take long for me to believe in what SBS stood for. To begin with, it had been thrown a crumb and operated on a shoestring, but ultimately it was an experiment that worked.

When the announcement of my new position was made public, the press was very kind to me. However, a number of ethnic community leaders thought my appointment strange. The Melbourne press had favoured Frank Galbally, the prominent Melbourne lawyer who had been associated with the planning of several ethnic and multicultural functions and had been closely involved in the setting up of SBS. One Melbourne newspaper referred to me as 'more Australian than the meat pie'. This sort of comment didn't worry me. I had been born and bred in Sydney; my grandparents had lived here; and, while I had grown up in a Lebanese environment, I felt and was Australian. It was rumoured that the then prime minister, Malcolm Fraser, had wanted Galbally for the position, and Ian Sinclair had wanted Bruce Gyngell, who was then managing director of

SBS Television; I was the third choice that they could actually agree upon. I had to go in cold, not knowing anything about the media. I ended up being chairman for nearly nineteen years, working under both Coalition and Labor governments.

On the day of the announcement of my appointment I called into SBS's offices in Sydney's Elizabeth Street and met, for the first time, the managing director, Ron Fowell, who was responsible for both radio and television, to get a feel of the organisation and its workings. When I visited the television studios, which was a tiny office with low ceilings, occupying one and a half floors, I thought it was really amateur hour.

SBS Radio had been on air for a couple of years. Broadcasting in just a handful of languages and staffed mainly by amateur broadcasters, the station was known as 2EA in Sydney and 3EA in Melbourne. Television on the UHF frequency, which as said before was most difficult to receive, even in Sydney and Melbourne, commenced a few months prior to my joining in 1981 and was known as Channel 0. SBS Television only got to air because of the fine planning and operating skills of that dynamic doyen of television in Australia, Bruce Gyngell, who achieved the feat in just eighteen months. Bruce had been given the brief to set up SBS Television by the Fraser government and he became manager of television. No one else could have set it up in such a short time. It was a great challenge, but Bruce enjoyed challenges. Television was beamed out of rented office space in Milsons Point, Sydney, and from a small office in Melbourne. SBS Radio operated out of the old studios of 2SM in Clarence Street, in Sydney, and from an office in Melbourne.

Because SBS was set up so quickly, many mistakes were made and it was certainly not done according to standard government operating procedures. Many short cuts were taken, all above board, but contrary to the way government works. It took years to sort it all out, and there was plenty of controversy along the way.

SBS was Mickey Mouse stuff compared to the ABC and the commercial stations. Gough Whitlam, as prime minister, had established SBS Radio; Malcolm Fraser, later prime minister, introduced the television service. Critics queued up to complain, saying it was a waste of taxpayers' money when only a very small section of Australia could receive the service. Some ethnic groups were critical because they weren't getting any, or sufficient, air time. Other groups who *had* air time criticised the radio broadcasters for not delivering what some communities wanted to hear. Everybody, it seemed, was a 'leader of their community'. In fact, getting and providing news from some of the warring countries resulted in us being accused of favouring some nations over others. Often we were receiving broadcasts from countries whose governments controlled and censored their media, to which many people took offence. It was my job to meet with all the communities, sit down and talk with them, and listen to their objections. They certainly gave me lots of advice.

I believe that radio, which gets closer to the people, is the main strength of SBS. We started off broadcasting in about seven or eight languages; today there are nearly seventy, and the broadcasters are highly professional.

Foreign material for television was very limited. Plus, it cost a great deal of money to purchase material. What our critics couldn't understand was that material for television had to be of a high and professional standard — we could only buy films that were of a high quality in terms of film type and sound. Many people seemed to have a relation who could get material cheaper than what we were paying, but often it was backyard-level filmmaking, and when we enquired if they had the rights to these films, the answer was always 'no'. Some people just weren't aware of the complexities of film distribution. The situation got so bad that complaints to the federal government led to the government calling in the federal police to investigate our purchasing procedures. I thought, 'How did I get into this?' It was a ridiculous situation. The police went to the great lengths to interview all the staff involved, but I was confident that everything was in order.

In 1983 I was in a London hotel after attending a rugby meeting and enjoying a pint of Guinness when I felt a tap on my shoulder. It was a stranger who identified himself as a Commonwealth law officer. He said that he was in London to investigate SBS's purchasing procedures after complaints had been made to the government by various ethnic communities. He assured me that everything was alright. Indeed, the complaints quietened down — the whole affair had been a waste of time and money. At the time, we had a London-based agent who was buying films for us, along with other contacts around the world. He assured me that there were no irregularities. The English company had a contract with us which specified the amount that they had to pay for films, and we handled all the finances from head office in Sydney. It was all completely above board.

Staff problems were common, and took up a great deal of my time in my early days with SBS, especially at the radio station. Many of the early employees there weren't experienced, whereas television was a lot more effective because most of the key positions were filled by trained people who had come from the ABC and the commercial stations. Bruce Gyngell was an excellent judge of potential talent. He promoted, from within, future SBS stalwarts George Donikian and Mary Kostakidis, who had had no previous experience on air. I had many arguments in defending Bruce's decisions to the board, who were mostly political appointees, many without media experience. Short cuts had to be taken in setting up SBS, more often than not bypassing the correct channels, which would have taken years. What Bruce was doing was out of the ordinary, and he didn't tolerate fools. I always had complete faith in his ability and judgment, and I knew that he could be trusted. I held him in the highest esteem. Whenever I could, in later years, I sent SBS managing directors to have a talk with Bruce. He was happy to assist them. You could always learn something about the media from Bruce Gyngell. He was widely respected.

One contentious incident involved TV transmitting towers. I was keen to have SBS's aerial attached to Channel Nine's tower so as to gain higher coverage and better reception. I went to see Channel Nine and we agreed on an amount that would see SBS be part of their tower. This was controversial among the board members, many of whom were inexperienced in business matters and viewed the whole idea as 'commercialisation'.

As I stated earlier, I have always believed that radio is the cornerstone of SBS and television the showcase; radio gets closer to the people — mothers could get information about babies and local community services, and the elderly who are housebound can hear information in their native language. SBS has always been at the crossroads, because many people in government did not appreciate what SBS represented. Most of them weren't able to receive it, in any case, and that may have exacerbated their frustration at government funds being spent on a service that was so inaccessible. From the time I began as chairman in 1981 until SBS received its charter in 1991, the constant question was, would it ever succeed?

In the 1986 federal budget, the Hawke Labor government announced that SBS would be amalgamated with the ABC. It was stated that this would save money. There was an uproar from the public, who participated in widespread demonstrations in most capital cities. In my opinion, the board of the ABC was only looking for a second television channel similar to the BBC to widen programming possibilities. David Hill, then chairman, and I could never see eye to eye, and I had a huge argument with the then minister, Michael Duffy, over the proposed selling out of SBS. If the amalgamation went through, it would be the end of SBS. I wasn't the most popular person with the minister, nor with David Hill.

I worked extremely hard to prevent the takeover, addressing the Labor Caucus Committee on the media and only receiving support from Jeannette McHugh, the incumbent member for the Sydney seat of Phillip. Things became quite unpleasant — even nasty. A committee was formed by the government to complete the amalgamation under the chairmanship of the then secretary of the department of communications, Charles Halton. At that stage, the Coalition parties showed no interest in stopping the amalgamation, and the Federation of Ethnic Community Councils Australia (FECCA) executive had discussions with the then leader of the Opposition, John Howard, who didn't give much hope of stopping the amalgamation. Many ethnic communities were protesting against the proposal, and meetings created heated debates all over Australia. One concession I achieved was equal representation of SBS and the ABC on the proposed board, after I was told that SBS would have only two board members out of twelve and that the managing director of SBS would play only a minor role.

During a parliamentary debate in 1986, Prime Minister Bob Hawke stated that when the amalgamation was complete, I would become its chairman. I was taken by surprise, as it was strongly rumoured at the time that David Hill was stepping down as chairman of the ABC in order to become managing director of the amalgamated broadcaster. I'm sure that we couldn't have worked together, as we were diametrically opposed on most things.

The amalgamation move was carried in the House of Representatives in 1987, but it then had to pass the Senate. We were all very nervous. To our surprise, the Conservatives opposed the proposal and, with the support of the Independents, defeated the bill. The good fight was over. I was overjoyed. David Hill duly became managing director of the ABC, and Ron Brown, managing director of SBS, later took the post of secretary of the Department of Immigration under the then minister, Mick Young. A few years later David Hill, as president of Australian Soccer and I as chairman of the SCG Trust locked horns once again.

Brian Johns became managing director of SBS, appointed by Minister Kim Beazley on the recommendation of a three-man selection panel, of which I was one. Both Brian and I worked extremely hard with the minister to make SBS an independent authority, on the same level as the ABC, and this was achieved when we gained our own charter in 1991. We could then appoint a managing director ourselves, without having to go through a laborious selection process via government channels, and make basic decisions without having to run to the government each time. SBS was here to stay.

The government attached certain conditions to the charter, one being advertising on television. Although we were basically opposed to advertising, Brian and I both felt that this was a small price to pay if we adopted strict guidelines. For example, there would be no more than five minutes of advertising per hour, and only before and after a program — during a natural break. We felt that we couldn't go to the government each year seeking funds when we had an opportunity to raise some revenue ourselves in a discreet way. I asked for guarantees if we proceeded with this proposal, one being that moneys collected wouldn't be deducted from our budget allocation. This was agreed to by the minister. The board of SBS accepted the recommendation and it has worked successfully. My main concern was to consolidate the position of SBS in our community. It was unique in the world, and worth preserving.

By the late 1980s, SBS was becoming more popular, and both radio and television receptions were being extended. In 1988, SBS Radio moved to very upmarket premises in Bondi Junction and became more professional. Each year it expanded into new areas and states, especially in the years when there was an election. It was always fashionable during an election campaign for SBS to be expanded into various electorates.

Brian Johns was drafted to head up the Australian Broadcasting Authority by the minister, Graham Richardson. Brian was very reluctant to go and I wasn't keen to lose him; however, apparently the then prime minister, Paul Keating, insisted. With this move the prime minister supported us with a grant of several million dollars to enable us to establish SBS Independent, which was to encourage Australian producers to come forward with joint ventures. This has turned out to be a tremendous success. It gives young and new producers opportunities that wouldn't have existed previously. Set up by Andy Lloyd James, SBS Independent has flourished and has aired some wonderful productions.

I always believed that SBS should have its own premises as a permanent head office in Sydney. As it was, we were spread over three areas in Sydney — the city, Milsons Point and Bondi Junction — and paying about $4 million in rent a year. With the permission of the government, and through the help of many friends who scouted properties and helped put the finances together, the SBS board settled on premises, in what was then a derelict building, in the lower North Shore suburb of Artarmon. The federal government granted us a loan of some $35 million, which would be paid back through the rent saved. This brought the whole organisation under one roof for the first time, and because we now had our charter, we could appoint our own managing director and not involve the minister. Malcolm Long, deputy managing director of the ABC, won the position and did a marvellous job. He developed a dedicated team that has gone from strength to strength. He was a tremendous asset to SBS and we were fortunate to have him.

With everyone under the one roof in our new premises, people were meeting each other for the first time and enjoying working in a more spacious environment. In the new television studios, you could now stand to be interviewed without bumping your head on the ceiling. Melbourne was to remain the only other city to have an SBS presence. The Melbourne team do a good job, and now that they have moved to new premises at South Melbourne's Federation Square, SBS will have a more prominent face in the centre of the city.

Over the years, the board became more professional and, as a result, SBS is now a highly sophisticated service. The government has granted SBS Radio extra AM bands and an additional FM band, and frequencies are now received all over Australia. Television has also expanded, and now only very few areas don't receive the service. SBS transmits from the ABC's transmission tower and there are now boosters throughout the country. Many country towns and cities adopted the self-help schemes and erected their own reception towers, raising funds by public subscription. Wagga Wagga, in the Riverina district of New South Wales, was the first town to do this. When I left SBS in 1999, about eighty Australian towns had followed its lead. SBS has now become part of the Australian fabric and there has been no more talk of amalgamation.

When pay television arrived in Australia in the early 1990s, we were in a very difficult position, not knowing whether we should go with the cable system or join the satellite service. At the time, there were various proposals put to government regarding licences for pay television. We were approached by many interested parties. I had several discussions with managing director Malcolm Long over the various alternatives. We reasoned that if we went with satellite, we could be left out in the cold if they didn't receive the licence, and vice versa.

One major concern was that another ethnic broadcaster could be set up — in fact, I was approached on many occasions about privatising SBS. We had an obligation to protect SBS. We came to the conclusion that ethnic communities were mostly interested in a news service. As a start, we then established the World News Service, bringing in a direct service from overseas broadcasters, both government and independent, free to air. We paid nothing for many of these services, and this allowed us to select items for the main news bulletins, saving us further money. It was a bonus.

Concerned that a commercial organisation could establish a service in direct opposition to us and force the cost of films and documentaries out of our reach, we decided that if the government would allow us to form a separate company with outside partners who would finance the organisation at no cost, SBS would package foreign films, subtitling them if necessary, and on-sell them to the pay TV organisations. This would allow us to control the purchasing of foreign films and also protect SBS from outside competition, ensuring that we maintained a strong base. A business plan was prepared and presented to the relevant government departments and, after a period of time, and answering many questions, we were given the green light to go ahead. We wouldn't be exposing the government to any financial risk.

Kerry Stokes, the major shareholder in Channel Seven and other business enterprises, came to see me and offered to finance the whole deal. I respected his opinion; however, I preferred to have a third partner. I thought that the further I could spread the interests, the better for SBS — in other words, the more input, the better.

Shortly after that meeting, I travelled to Egypt with a programmer to look at film distribution deals, and then on to London. There I received a message from an old rugby friend, Tony O'Reilly, now Sir Anthony. He said that he had heard I was coming to London and had therefore arranged for a driver to pick me up and take me to spend the weekend with him. I wasn't sure of the destination but soon found myself at Ascot racecourse, where one of Tony's companies, Waterford Crystal, was holding a race meeting. He had flown in from his holiday home in Cork, in southern Ireland, to present the trophy. After the races we boarded Tony's private jet and flew to Cork. During the flight, I surprised him by presenting him with our business plan. I carried that plan everywhere, as I never knew who I was going to meet! Before we landed, Tony said that his Australian company, Australian Provincial Newspapers, would like to be part of the consortium. He was happy with Kerry Stokes as a third partner, and this view was reciprocated.

On my return to Australia, PAN television was born, and this has become a great success. More importantly, it has secured SBS in the pay television market. PAN rented premises within SBS and beamed the World Movie Channel across Australia. The film rights deals also included broadcasting on SBS. The company still operates very successfully.

During my years with SBS I experienced some very sad occasions. I was especially saddened by the death of Robert Stokes, my right-hand man and the head of human resources. Robert was a person I respected and depended on greatly. I knew I would miss his loyalty and sturdy advice. He was, without doubt, the most respected person in the SBS organisation, and had been there since its birth. I could be a bit outspoken and impatient at times as board chairman, and Robert would calm things down by saying, 'Why don't we approach it in *this* manner?'

In 1997, Malcolm Long's five-year term as managing director was coming to an end. He was keen to do other things, including working overseas and forming his own consultancy. He had built a great team, he was a pleasure to work with, and he left SBS in a very good state. Malcolm was excellent at his job and, in my opinion, he should have been appointed managing director of the ABC when Brian Johns retired.

The board met to decide Malcolm's successor and determined that we needed a person who could project the organisation further through the media, making the public more aware of SBS. We needed

SPECIAL BROADCASTING SERVICE, 1981–99

a marketing person. We instructed the recruitment consultants to give us four candidates after they had sorted through all the applicants. We didn't know who had applied and who hadn't. The consultants duly recommended four candidates to the board's subcommittee, which comprised Nick Massinello, deputy chairman, Irene Moss, board member and at the time New South Wales ombudsman, and myself. If we didn't find the right person among these four candidates, we would call for the other applicants to be considered.

The usual suspects in the ethnic communities had a field day singling me out and accusing me of being prejudiced against some of the applicants, some of whom were former employees of SBS. They wanted me to stand down from the panel. Their accusations were false, of course, since I was at arm's length from the initial selection process, and, when confronted, they would invariably duck for cover. Nigel Milan, who had sat on the PAN board, was strongly recommended by the consultants and ended up winning the position. He was the ideal person to promote SBS. Nigel had a tremendous background in electronic media, both in Australia and New Zealand, at 2UE, 2GB, Channel Nine and PAN. I thought his profile was too high for the job, but in the interview he was most impressive and was prepared to take a drop in salary. He believed in the SBS concept. Nigel performed the job at the highest level and implemented all the board's policies. With Chris Sharp, who took over Robert Stokes's position as head of policy, Peter Kavanagh, head of television, Quang Luu, head of radio, and Maureen Crow, head of human resources, this developed into a highly respected and dedicated team.

My retirement in 1999, after nearly nineteen years as chairman, gave me the chance to reflect on a wonderful experience with great people supporting me, especially when times were tough and we were working together under extreme difficulties. It seemed that SBS was always at the crossroads. Several years ago, I was approached by a merchant banker and a prominent businessman who suggested that they could privatise SBS. My reaction was that I would be out in front leading the fight to defy this. SBS has been referred to as 'the little Aussie battler', and it has been a privilege to have been a part of its development. SBS is indeed a unique

I am honoured to have received this investiture for contribution to multiculturalism as chairman of Special Broadcasting Service: a D. Lit (Hon) from the University of Western Sydney. With me are the chancellor, Sir Ian Turbett, and the vice-chancellor, Professor Janice Reid.

organisation. It truly reflects the multicultural society that Australia is, and has played an important role in framing our tolerant society.

When I left SBS, Prime Minister John Howard wrote the following words of my term as chairman to be read out at my farewell:

It is with a mixture of pleasure and sadness that I provide a farewell message for Sir Nicholas Shehadie as he ends his term as chairman of SBS.

As chairman of SBS for eighteen years, Sir Nicholas has led SBS for most of its existence and has steered it through some significant changes. Under Sir Nicholas's leadership, SBS has expanded from its origins in the early 1970s as an experimental ethnic radio station based in Sydney and Melbourne, to a comprehensive radio and television network ready to meet the needs of the whole of Australia in the new millennium. SBS now provides a full range of programming; it supports the development of skilled employment in the Australian film and broadcast industry; and the creation of SBS Independent cements the organisation's role as a key supporter of new Australian film.

Sir Nicholas has been instrumental in building the integrity of the reporting services of SBS. He has also created an organisation ready to meet its dual roles as national broadcaster and commercial business. In meeting its charter, SBS has developed a range of distinctive programming to inform and entertain. With audiences of up to six million a week, SBS has moved from being the provider of niche programs to providing a genuine alternative to commercial television. SBS has created markets for new services that have allowed it to reduce its demands on the public purse.

I am pleased to say that Sir Nicholas Shehadie's greatest contribution to Australia has been in raising the awareness of all Australians regarding the value of our multicultural society. Whether as captain of the Wallabies or as chairman of SBS, Sir Nicholas has shown us that the synergy of the parts makes for a more dynamic whole. Today's SBS is a product of that vision. We have all been fortunate to have Sir Nicholas as a champion of Australia's diversity, and his achievements and vision provide us all with the courage and perseverance to nurture that unique Australian identity.

It is important that the current and future boards of SBS recognise that they are in the previleged position of operating a service for the Australian community and not a business.

15 SOME THOUGHTS ON MULTICULTURALISM

Immigrants have made a tremendous contribution to the development of Australia in many fields, including politics, business, medicine, the arts and sport. At my school in Redfern I had many friends with varying ethnic origins. Although I was often the victim of racist taunts — I was called 'Midnight' and 'Black Nick', among other names — it never occurred to me that I was different or less of an Australian than my schoolmates.

Later, during my international rugby days, I always found it strange when biographical details in programs would identify me as 'Nick Shehadie of Lebanese descent'. My team-mates were never described as being of Irish, English, Welsh or Scottish descent. Today most countries have so-called 'foreigners' in their national rugby teams.

My reflections on multiculturalism and its benefits were expressed in a speech I delivered to the Capricornia Institute of Higher Education in Rockhampton, Queensland, several years ago. In this chapter, I want to revisit some of the points and conclusions I raised.

The multiculturalism of Australia is not a new phenomenon. It has been part of the very essence of Australia's development from the earliest beginnings, acknowledged in the history of the Australian people when the first Aborigines and Torres Strait Islanders emigrated here from across the seas.

In 1788, a new wave of settlers made the second major impact on this ancient land some 19 000 kilometres from their Anglo-Celtic origins. Immigrants — some forced, some voluntary — began the stream of settlement which has continued unabated to the present day and which, in the second part of the last century, was joined and strengthened by new streams from all the European cultures, from the Middle East, from Asia, and from the Pacific.

Australia, undeniably, is a nation of immigrants, who provide much of our nation's strength. The inspiration and determination of each wave of new settlers has woven their own contribution into the rich tapestry of this unique land.

It is ironic that there are some who would deny this concept of multiculturalism which so extensively permeates Australian society already. It is futile to reject the notion and philosophy of multiculturalism, for this is a reality that has arisen from Australia's history of settlement and development.

The Australian census figures of 1901, when Australia became a federation, are illuminating given the considerable limitations of travel and of communication at that time. The 22 per cent of the population regarded as having been born outside of Australia indicated considerable ethnic and cultural diversity: Europeans, Asians, Pacific Islanders, Africans, and North and South Americans. Of these, and including the estimated indigenous population at that time of about 90 000, some 27 per cent of the population came from a non-English-speaking background.

Surely multiculturalism as a policy requires no debate; what can and should be debated is how to make it work better, in the interests of our great country's development.

The policy of multiculturalism recognises the fact of diversity in Australia and the socially enriching value of that diversity. Its purpose is to promote unity and cohesion. A multicultural Australia is one in which all citizens have an equal right to participate in all aspects of the nation's life.

Three aspects of multiculturalism are emphasised in the policies of all Commonwealth governments, past and present: respect for cultural difference, social justice, and economic efficiency.

We should continue to press for the cultural dimension that all Australians should be free to develop, adapt and express elements of their individual cultural heritage within the unifying framework of a commitment to Australia, and its laws and institutions. But diversity doesn't make a country multicultural, nor does food, quaint customs or folkloric festivals — these are the by-products, not the substance.

True multiculturalism is a dynamic diversity whose dimensions encompass social justice and true equality, where every voice has a right to be heard, and is listened to with respect. Multiculturalism is about rights and opportunities — the rights of everyone to develop their own unique identity, woven from strands of the richness of the old and the brilliance of the new — opportunities to benefit from and contribute to everything this source has to offer, without being compelled to surrender identity, nor to suffer discrimination.

Despite these universal ideals of justice and autonomy, some opponents of multiculturalism have presented it as divisive and negative. Indeed, the reverse is true. Australia has suffered far less inter-ethnic and racial strife than other multicultural countries with different social models. It has continued to inspire a commitment to Australia by members of all ethnic groups.

The basis of this policy is clear: multiculturalism is not about entrenching divisions. It is about accepting differences — in the same way that political democracy accommodates the expression of a diversity of views.

The social dimension means that the structures and processes of Australian society should acknowledge and be responsive to the diversity of its population. People's life chances shouldn't be affected by their ethnicity, race, religion, language or place of birth. Conformity to a particular cultural stereotype shouldn't be the price demanded in return for equal treatment or the right to participate fully in society.

The economic dimension of multiculturalism means that Australia should be able to make effective use of all the nation's human resources. This is particularly necessary in the current economic environment. Australia's future standard of living depends on increased efficiency and competitiveness. To achieve this, we need to derive the best from all members of our workforce, whether born here or overseas.

Multicultural policy embraces such issues as the provision of appropriate retraining arrangements for those manufacturing industries with large immigrant workforces who are facing the challenge of competition and technological change; increasing the school retention rates of Aboriginal Australians and certain ethnic groups; effectively managing a multicultural, multilingual workforce; making better use of the education, skills and entrepreneurial ability of immigrants by teaching English and recognising and encouraging the many overseas qualifications to reach our Australian standards; and maintaining and developing the language resources of our nation in order to advance Australia's trade and tourism interests.

Such concerns go to the heart of contemporary economic priorities. They recognise that the cultural diversity of Australia isn't a problem. Rather, it provides us with assets that can help to secure our future in an increasingly competitive world.

Having focused on contemporary issues, let's review the factors that have influenced where we are today.

The British contributions are acknowledged and recognised as providing some of the most dominant characteristics of Australian society, the foundations on which so much of our governmental and public-sector developments have grown. Perhaps some of the quality of formality and structure from this British tradition may not have been understood as clearly as other cultural streams. Contributions of the Irish have provided a unique influence on traditional bonds of family and mateship; on a larrikin sense of fun, streaked with irreverence and anti-authoritarianism (which other countries might deem impudent). Such characteristics of the earlier settlers have now become an intrinsic part of the Australian persona and have been immortalised in our literature and music. And, by a similar process, cultures from all parts of the world are meeting in a dynamic panorama and being integrated into an ever-evolving Australian identity.

Early in the twentieth century, many new immigrants were exploited for their labour, for their willingness to work hard and for long hours. In a sense, they continued the pioneering work of the early convicts and settlers in developing and extending the frontiers of the land which established a sound economic base for the nation, whether it was in the mines, on the farms, on the railways, in the cane fields, in the desert or in the Snowy Mountains.

Since the 1940s, Australia has opened its gates to immigrants as never before — immigrants who have come from the ravages of war, from brutal discrimination, from genocidal regimes and from the refugee experience. These epic experiences of man's inhumanity to man of so many of our more recent immigrants have added a further dimension to Australia's social and cultural history and strengthened our claims to mature nationhood.

Many components of a multicultural policy have been implemented across the nation at all levels of government. Clearly, governments have done a great deal to assist the immigrant. What can and should the immigrant do for Australia?

Of primary importance is that the laws of the land should, and must, be accepted. Differences within nationalities have no place in the new land. Immigrants have voluntarily chosen to make Australia their new home, and the Australian way of life should be respected. It is regrettable that inter-ethnic discrimination between immigrants has surfaced on occasions — Middle Eastern and Asian youths being a recent example where aggressive rivalry has resulted. This is not the Australian way.

Ethnicity doesn't of itself create violence. Rather, the experience of disadvantage, inequity, perceived inferiority and boredom are the flames that can ignite when the young are overwhelmed by a sense of powerlessness and hopelessness. There is no insistence on any one group that their individual culture should be forgotten. Tolerance, support and acceptance must predominate.

I have written this book on the eve of a potentially dark time for our country, and for the world. The twenty-first century has ushered in horrendous acts of terrorism on our own doorstep. It is my wish that our leaders and communities will find a way forward by promoting tolerance, goodwill and humanitarianism, and in doing so preserve the essence of multiculturalism and the unique Australian way of life.

16 A FINAL WORD

I was created a knight bachelor in January 1976. This was a complete surprise and I was humbled. In 1999, I decided to retire from public life when my wife, Professor Marie Bashir, was appointed governor of New South Wales. My health had suffered some setbacks over recent years and I felt it was an appropriate time to return to private life, which would also allow me to spend more time with my family and grandchildren.

I hope that, by reading this book, my grandchildren will learn something from my early years spent growing up during the Depression, and about how one can surmount any adversity if one has a family unit in which each member supports the others. It is said that the strength of the family unit is disappearing from our society today. That is sad, because I would hope that families continue to make a contribution to the development of this wonderful country, indeed to the world at large.

Growing up, we were always taught that everyone is equal. Some do it harder than others, but never lose their self-respect. The Shehadies have always shunned the use of the words 'I can't'; They don't exist in our vocabulary. I was privileged to come from a united family, which became even more united after my father passed away at a relatively young age. My mother was the matriarch and the driving force for all of us, and instilled in me a committed sense of values. It has certainly been a life worth living.

APPENDIX 1

RUGBY COACHES — I'VE KNOWN A FEW

During my representative rugby career, I played under a number of coaches. They varied from the type of coach who would yell at you to get you to do something, to those who just had a quiet word in your ear and gave you a pat on the back. I always responded best to the latter type.

On my tours, it was always the assistant manager who was responsible for coaching duties, although a notable exception occurred on the 1947–48 tour of the British Isles, France and North

America when Arnold Tancred was both tour manager and coach, sharing the latter duties with the tour captain, Bill McLean. Jeff Noseda toured as team secretary, handling day-to-day issues as well as general correspondence. Arnold and Bill were extremely tough, and training was very physical.

On my first Wallaby tour to New Zealand, Bill Cerutti did the hard work and Trevor Allan had an important input. On a subsequent New Zealand tour, Bill Cerutti was assistant manager once again, and he and the captain, John Solomon, did most of the coaching, as did Jock Blackwood later. On the South African tour of 1953, Johnny Wallace was the coach, with John Solomon also directing much of the training operation. On the 1957–58 tour of the British Isles, Dave Cowper, the assistant manager, was coach and relied heavily on the captain, Bob Davidson. That tour was nowhere near as successful as the other tours.

I found Wally Meagher to be my most successful coach, both at the Randwick Club and when he took over the Australian team in 1954. Prior to the Wallabies leaving for South Africa in 1953, it was Wally who ran the team, and his patient and sincere approach made every player feel important. He was very shrewd tactician who never missed a trick.

I found 'Jika' Travers very technical and inclined to be full of theory on what to do after the game. On one occasion, we were training prior to an All Blacks match in Sydney and Jika stood at the gate leading onto the field at Sydney University, handing out slips of paper to the players as we passed through. Jack Baxter, the tough, rugged front-row forward from the Eastern Suburbs Club, read aloud what Jika had written him: 'You are rucking too hard.' Jack shook his head and said, 'Do you want me to play in sandshoes?'

Barney Walsh was the most energetic coach I played under; he was never short of a word and was very noisy.

I tried to follow Wally Meagher's style of coaching when, on my retirement, I coached South Harbour, who defeated the touring Fijians, and St John's College at Sydney University, who won the inter-collegiate rugby competition. I always felt that a coach needed to use a variety of training routines mixed in with a little fun.

There were certainly many fine coaches on the international scene during my playing days: Fred Allen and Vic Cavanagh of New Zealand, Carwyn James of Wales, and Danie Craven of South Africa, just to name a few. During my subsequent term as president of the Australian Rugby Union, I got to know three very high-profile Australian coaches — Bob Templeton of Queensland and the New South Welshmen Bob Dwyer and Alan Jones. Templeton was greatly admired by his players. He was a man with a father image: if he was highly successful on the field with those rugged and committed Queensland Reds, he was even more successful off the field, in the manner in which he treated his players.

Bob Dwyer and Alan Jones, who for a period displaced him, both enjoyed triumphs with Australian teams, recording World Cup and Grand Slam victories, respectively. They were similar in many respects, fairly technical and taking advantage of the greater access to electronic devices that had become available. At all times, these two men had the respect of their teams, and as ARU president they always had my full support. At no time did I hear even a whisper of criticism of their control over the teams they handled. I think Alan Jones, a peerless and inspirational orator, signalled his arrival on the scene when he guided the Manly Club to an upset grand final victory over the Ella-led perennial Sydney winners, Randwick. In 1984, Jones took the Wallabies to the United Kingdom to create perhaps the finest conquest in Australian rugby history. This was referred to as rugby at its finest, with Mark Ella 'marshalling a flat back line that bewitched British defences'. The four internationals won comfortably against Ireland, Scotland, Wales and England.

Reinstated as national coach, Bob Dwyer was to achieve his own summit success, the momentous World Cup victory in Britain in 1991. That triumph hung in the balance at Lansdowne Road where the unpredictable Irish took the lead, with victory in sight until Michael Lynagh, in the closing seconds, scored a last-ditch winning try for the Wallabies, leaving, as one critic said, the Irish to cry into their Guinness. (Wales was beaten 38 to 3.) A glorious Campese try buried the New Zealand All Blacks, and the Webb Ellis trophy was ours with a thumping 12 to 6 victory over England at Twickenham.

Bob Dwyer subsequently wrote a book, appropriately titled *Winning Ways*, in which he reveals a remarkable insight into his coaching make-up. He wrote of commentators who spoke of Australia playing with a flair in attack and an expansive, fifteen-man game, which he said produced a false image in people's minds. He recalled that he once said he wouldn't like the type of rugby Australia plays to be likened to a frilly evening dress. He would much prefer it to be likened to a well-tailored suit, cut with precision from the best cloth, nicely structured and devoid of any trimmings. In other words, textbook rugby: sharp, neat, efficient, structured. Dwyer must be the game's greatest optimist, because he confesses to telephoning Michael Lynagh a year before the World Cup and telling him to have a glass of champagne 'to celebrate our victory'.

Ken Catchpole once asked Bob Dwyer how it was possible for one person to coach a whole team, since the coach couldn't possibly know everything there was to know about every position. He replied that he knew some things about all positions and a lot of things about some positions. A wise coach, he maintained, has to keep learning, and developing his tactics, if only to prevent the opposition knowing what to expect. Coaches should be prepared to use whatever resources are available, he said, even it if means going outside rugby, and he cited his invitation in 1991 to the fierce-tackling Rugby League forward, Terry Randall, to come and lecture his players. Dwyer believes that the most common fault of coaches is that they aren't demanding enough. He once told his assistant coaches at Randwick that they weren't running a child-minding service two nights a week.

A modest man, Dwyer says in his book that he doesn't over-estimate the value of a coach's contribution to a team's performance.

> If there are fifteen players on the field and one coach on the sideline, then I consider the coach's input to be about one sixteenth of the total, or about seven per cent. This isn't false modesty. I genuinely believe that this is about the extent of a coach's influence on a top-level team's performance. At the

same time, I do think that a contribution of this size can have a critical bearing on how a team performs.

There is no doubt that, in modern rugby, the role of the coach has changed dramatically. In my day, the coach was a lone figure out there on the training paddock, calling from time to time to consult with his captain, and fulfilling the challenging duties of confessor, trainer, doctor and psychologist. Today our coaches have an entire entourage at their disposal, comprising fitness trainers, back coaches, forward coaches, tackling coaches, dietitians, psychologists, and so on ... there are more chiefs than Indians! Under strict international board rules during the amateur days, we would only assemble two days before a home game to prepare, but today the players and their families go into camp at five-star resorts for a week or more. Times certainly are changing.

APPENDIX 2

MY IDEAL FIRST FIFTEEN

From time to time, I have been asked by rugby enthusiasts to select a team comprised of the greatest players I played against in international football. Not an easy task. In the eleven years I was in the Test arena, there were many changing faces in the opposition and many great ones among them. So many, in fact, that I could probably choose two fifteens of equal calibre.

So, what makes a great footballer? In my eyes, a number of key ingredients combine to justify the accolade, but foremost for me is the player who gives 100 per cent effort right until the final whistle blows; a player who is super-fit, totally committed and possesses that touch of magic needed to pull off the unexpected. He's the player, recognised by the crowded grandstands, who unfailingly brings the fans to their feet.

Here is the team I have chosen. It would be the ideal team to coach! I'm sure it will create some controversy, but I have chosen this line-up without fear or favour.

BOB SCOTT (New Zealand — full-back). The supreme custodian with pace, a superb goal-kicking boot and a reliable defender. What a gift! He had a tactical flair that enabled him to chime into the back line with precision timing.

TONY O'REILLY (Ireland — winger). Glamour wing-three-quarter, big-strider with devastating pace and swerve off either foot. Highly dangerous close to the goal line, and everywhere a crowd favourite. His on-field performance was only exceeded by his off-field good humour.

RON JARDEN (New Zealand — winger). One of the speediest wingers I played against, and a real match winner. Dangerous with the ball in hand or on the boot and a prolific point-scorer for the All Blacks.

JOHNNY SMITH (New Zealand — centre). The most complete centre I have seen in action. Nuggety in build, his big hips, which he used to perfection, made him a difficult target to tackle. A Maori champion. Quick hands and a turn of speed.

BLEDDYN WILLIAMS (Wales — centre). Similar in build to Johnny Smith (see previous page), a solid defender and blessed with quick hands that enabled him to make clever breaks. Williams was a master tactician on the field.

CLIFF MORGAN (Wales — five-eighth). Welsh wizard, small in stature but dynamic as a fine organiser and with a positional sense that always had him in the right spot. This will-o'-the-wisp could read the game beautifully.

HAYDN TANNER (Wales — half-back). Played for Wales while still a schoolboy; a Welsh legend before the Second World War and immediately afterwards. This powerful 14-stoner (90 kilograms) was a great ball distributor and could tackle as fiercely as a back-row forward. He was the tallest half-back I played against.

JEAN PRAT (France — flanker). Acknowledged as the player who put French rugby on the map. 'Monsignor Rugby', the French called him. Captain of France and a 51-Test campaigner, he was a fine leader and a mobile player who was never off the ball.

PETER ROBBINS (England — flanker). Strong, fast and very fit, he was the bane of our 1957–58 Wallaby tour. A smart tactician and great attacker who could fill any position in the back line when needed.

HENNIE MULLER (South Africa — number eight). Tagged 'The Whippet', he was probably the fastest forward to take the field for the Springboks. A glorious cover defender who destroyed the All Blacks on their 1949 tour to the Republic, he was the perfectly equipped back-rower.

COLIN MEADS (New Zealand — number eight). Known as 'Pine Tree', he stood just under two metres tall, a giant who controlled the lineouts, rucks and mauls in intimidating fashion. A rival not to be messed with.

SALTY du RAND (South Africa — second-rower). Tall and raw-boned, a fine lineout jumper and solid as a rock in general play. A tiger in the tight work and, for a big man, highly mobile.

JOHN SIMPSON (New Zealand — front-rower). The 'Prince of Props' with extraordinary strength, as befits a former heavyweight boxing champion. He never took a backward step and was mentor to many props in the art of scrummaging.

KEVIN SKINNER (New Zealand — front-rower). They came no tougher. A powerful scrummager, he excelled in the tight play and led by example. He was tutored by Simpson and brought out of retirement to counteract the South Africans.

KARL MULLEN (Ireland — hooker). Fast striker of the ball, good around the paddock, a veritable ferret pirating the ball out of the rucks and, overall, a wonderful leader and tactician.

Apologies to some very fine players who missed a jersey in my line-up: Don Clarke (New Zealand), Ken Jones (Wales), Jack Kyle (Ireland), Eric Evans (England), Tom Kemp (England), David Marques (England), Rex Willis (Wales), Wilson Whineray (New Zealand), Has Catley (New Zealand), Guy Basquet (France), Jaap Becker (South Africa) and Jack Matthews (Wales). What a star-studded reserve bench!

Six overseas tours and some thirty Tests brought me close to many of the Australian players during my playing era. At the risk of leaning a little to our great 1947–48 tour party, this is my ideal Australian line-up from during my career.

BRIAN PIPER (NSW — full-back). Rock of Gibraltar, a full-back who had a superb knack of making the extra man and probing the gap. A sound defender, blessed with the safest of hands, and a reliable goal-kicker to boot.

CHARLES EASTES (NSW — winger). A rangy, good-natured fellow who spelt danger with the ball in his hands. High-stepping and speedy, Eastes was one of the finest wingers I played with. An exciting tour of the British Isles was cut short when he broke his wrist at Newport.

EDDIE STAPLETON (NSW — winger). Not the speediest winger to play for Australia, but certainly one of the most effective. Big in stature, rugged in play, and quite fearless — Stapleton could be a match winner.

TREVOR ALLAN (NSW — centre). I doubt that I ever laid eyes on a better defending centre who also excelled in attack. He performed many try-saving tackles, most memorably in our 1948 Test defeat of England at Twickenham. Few better leaders.

JOHN SOLOMON (NSW — centre). Quick enough to play centre or wing, equipped with a skilful swerve and sharp acceleration when a gap appeared. Much admired for his astute captaincy.

ARTHUR SUMMONS (NSW — five-eighth). Tough, diminutive pivot and a slick runner with the ball when an opening appeared. He set up outside backs with reliable service. Summons later became a prominent professional League player.

CYRIL BURKE (NSW — half-back). Size was no handicap for this Newcastle master half-back, certainly the best I played with in my career. He had the biggest sidestep I ever saw from any player, delivered quick-fire service from the scrums and rucks, and had a keen eye for a possible gap.

BILL McLEAN (QLD — flanker). McLean brought his former commando skills onto the rugby field. A tough, hard-hitting forward who led by example, he was speedy around the field and a huge punt kicker of the ball.

COLIN WINDON (NSW — flanker). As back-row forwards go, he was the very best. A try-scoring machine, a superb attacker and with the speed of a three-quarter, the man they nicknamed 'Breeze' was simply peerless in supporting play.

ARTHUR BUCHAN (NSW — number eight). Uncompromising tackler, fine cover defender, and blessed with a powerful frame from his surf club days. A true eighty-minute performer.

GRAEME COOKE (QLD — second-rower). This remarkable forward played his first Test in 1933 on the tour to South Africa and his last Test in 1948, a span that spoke volumes for his fitness, durability and power play. He was a simply magnificent lineout jumper.

DON KRAEFFT (NSW — second-rower). Rangy and agile Sydney University product, he was highly mobile and a fine two-handed lineout jumper. Kraefft teamed with Cooke as a powerhouse second-row pair for the 1947–48 tourists.

ERIC TWEEDALE (NSW — front-rower). Extremely mobile for a prop forward, valuable in the lineouts and a sturdy worker in the tight stuff.

TONY MILLER (NSW — front-rower). Strong-man scrummager who did his best work in the tight, with willing contribution to lineouts. He was a good man to have on your side.

KEN KEARNEY (NSW — hooker). The premier hooker during my playing career. Short and solid in build, he had no fear and was mobile around the paddock. Kearney went on to make a big name for himself in Rugby League.

Apologies again to such accomplished players as Alan Cameron, Dick Tooth, John Thornett, Jim Phipps, Terry Curley, Keith Cross, Rex Mossop, Neville Cottrell, Des Connor, Herb Barker, Bob McMaster, Kevin Ryan and Rod Phelps. They all wore the Wallaby jumper with pride.

INDEX